D0592356

The Puritan Conscience and Modern Sexuality

The Puritan Conscience and Modern Sexuality

EDMUND LEITES

Yale University Press
New Haven and London

Designed by Susan P. Fillion
and set in Trump Medieval type by Eastern Graphics.
Printed in the United States of America by BookCrafters,
Inc., Chelsea, Michigan.

Library of Congress Cataloging-in-Publication Data

Leites, Edmund, 1939–
    The Puritan conscience and modern sexuality.

    Bibliography: p.
    Includes index.
    1. Sexual ethics—England—History—17th century.
2. Sexual ethics—England—History—18th century.
3. Puritans—England—History. I. Title.
HQ32.L42 1986   305.3'.0942   85-20198
ISBN 0-300-03490-3 (alk. paper)

*The paper in this book meets the guidelines for perma-
nence and durability of the Committee on Production
Guidelines for Book Longevity of the Council on Library
Resources.*

10 9 8 7 6 5 4 3 2 1

For Fred Lipschitz, Rochelle Slovin, and Silvan Tomkins

Tirelessly the process of thinking makes
new beginnings, returning in a roundabout way
to its original object.

Walter Benjamin
The Origin of German Tragic Drama

Contents

Acknowledgments

My thanks go first and foremost to Amy Waterman, whose editorial skills were essential to the completion of this book. I also thank the PSC-CUNY Research Award Program of the City University of New York for its generous financial support.

The research for chapters 1 and 4 was undertaken mostly at the Library of the Union Theological Seminary in New York City, and much of the writing of these chapters was done there as well. Often it seemed like a second home.

An earlier version of chapter 2 was read to the University Seminar on Content and Methods in the Social Sciences, Columbia University, in March 1978. I have been a member of this seminar for over a decade, and I particularly wish to acknowledge the help given to me by its longtime chairman, Joseph Maier, and by two of its devoted members, Rhoda Metraux and Werner Cahnman.

Martin Wangh, who cochaired the Interdisciplinary Colloquium on the Social Sciences and Psychoanalysis at the New York Psychoanalytic Institute, pressed me to consider what Locke did *not* consider in his thinking about parents' love of their children. Paul Desjardins of Haverford College reminded me of the importance of civic spirit to Locke.

I began chapters 3 and 5 while an Andrew W. Mellon Fellow at the William Andrews Clark Memorial Library at UCLA in July 1978 and March 1979; chapter 3 was largely completed at the Institute for Advanced Study in Princeton in 1979 and 1980. I benefited from the well-known and gracious hospitality of both institutions.

Louis Mink astutely called my attention to the difference between the expression of emotion and the venting of feelings when I read an earlier version of chapter 3 at the Center for the Humanities of Wesleyan University in March 1980.

Silvan Tomkins, in frequent conversations, has become my beloved teacher and friend. Chapters 3 and 5 in particular owe much to his analysis of the emotions. Eli Sagan has encouraged me throughout much of the writing of this book; his sense of the moral and psychological meaning of social forms reinforced my own belief in the worth of research into these matters.

My ventures into sixteenth- and seventeenth-century cultural history were prompted by Benjamin Nelson's studies of the philosophical and sociological significance of conscience and casuistry in early modern Europe. Ben and I talked together from the time I was a teenager at his homes in New York City, Stony Brook, and Montauk, at his office at the New School for Social Research, and at the many conferences we attended, and sometimes organized, together. These discussions, and his many articles, gave me a first idea of how historical research might serve philosophical purposes.

Chapter 5 owes much to conversations with Max Novak, of UCLA, whose work on the theatre of late-seventeenth- and early-eighteenth-century England reflects his understanding of the lively sexuality found in the best comedies of the period.

My longtime association with Vytautas Kavolis, as a fellow officer of the International Society for the Comparative Study of Civilizations and as my coeditor of the *Comparative Civilizations Review*, deepened my conviction that the formation and organization of feelings is an appropriate subject for the philosopher as well as for the historian and sociologist.

The ideas on hierarchy expressed in chapter 6 owe much to Louis Dumont, of the Ecole des Hautes Etudes en Sciences Sociales in Paris. Jean-Claude Galey, also of the Ecole, urged me to strengthen an earlier, and much weaker, version of the chapter. Roberto Schwarz, of the Universidade Estadual de Campinas, similarly insisted—in one of my visits to Brazil which he kindly arranged—that I develop the ideas of this chapter more imaginatively and fully. Conversations about chapter 6 with my father, Nathan Leites, gave me the courage to go on with the enterprise, as he has done so often in our talks. My old and dear friend Jacob Taubes, of the Freie Universität Berlin, invited me to present my work to his seminar in January 1982, where the insightful and sympathetic response was encouraging. One of the members of that seminar, Heinz-Dieter Kittsteiner, has become a friend and intellectual companion. His work on the history of conscience and casuistry from Luther to Kant crystallized my sense that the key term in my own work on the history of conscience was *constancy*.

The final drafts of this book were much improved by the criticisms of Paul Robinson of Stanford University and Vern Bullough of the State University College at Buffalo. Robinson asked me to consider how my own work stands in relation to Foucault's, and Bullough saved me from several exaggerations. I thank Sue Allen-Mills of Cambridge University Press and Jeanne Ferris of Yale University Press as well for their editorial comments. And if the prose of this book has any virtue, it is due largely to the revisions suggested by a woman of many virtues, Rochelle Slovin.

Introduction

The subject of this book is constancy—or, rather, the ethic of constancy as it developed in seventeenth- and eighteenth-century English culture. Of course, questions about the meaning and value of emotional and moral constancy are not original to the seventeenth and eighteenth centuries. They are already issues of some importance in classical Greek philosophy, notably in Platonic and Stoic ethics, and they remain a topic of importance in medieval and Renaissance moral philosophy, both Christian and Jewish. I have chosen the seventeenth and eighteenth centuries in England as the focus of my research because they mark a decisive turning point in the history of the topic: the point at which the grand movement of morals, commonly called Puritan, began to transform "merrie old England" into a more sober and steady world. The thoroughness of the Puritan demand for emotional and moral constancy in various areas of life— in all areas of life, finally—is remarkable, as is the degree to which this demand extended outward toward all classes of society.

Although the demand for constancy was not unique to seventeenth-century Puritans, the Puritans are especially important in the study of constancy in the seventeenth and eighteenth centuries in England because they put constancy very much at the center of their own moral vision. They saw self-control, sobriety, and the unremitting pursuit of one's spiritual and moral goals as major and necessary expressions of religious seriousness and consciousness of God. Not all Puritans felt this way, however. Christopher Hill, in particular, has stressed the antinomian or free-spirit element in the Puritan tradition as it is found, for example, in the Ranters and those associated with the Family of Love. If this antinomian element is carried far enough, the demand for constancy takes a back seat to an ethic which requires acting according to the movement of one's spirit. But what one might call the mainstream of Puritanism did make moral constancy a core virtue.

In his *Protestant Ethic and the Spirit of Capitalism*, Max Weber wrote that Puritanism "attempted to subject man to the supremacy of a purposeful will, to bring his actions under constant self-control with a careful consideration of their ethical consequences. . . . This active self-control . . . was also the most important practical idea of Puritanism. . . . [It] tried to enable a man to maintain and act upon his constant motives."[1] The Puritans did not limit this concern to a few areas of life. In marriage, public life, commerce, child-raising, religious behavior, and even war, they demanded emotional steadiness and self-control. Their distinctive, highly elaborated ethic of constancy became a new standard which later generations of English culture developed, opposed, or in some way attempted to modify.

Yet it would be altogether incorrect to say that the Puritans were not emotional. They were not "cold fish." It is in their idea of marriage, in particular, that we see their desire to integrate constancy with emotional spontaneity. It is easy enough to associate constancy with a strict and repressive attitude allowing for no movement of the heart. An image comes to mind of the severe Stoic choking down all feelings to maintain his iron composure. This image is unfair to many of the Stoic philosophers who took the part of constancy, and it certainly would not apply to the Puritan idea of constancy within marriage. The ministers who called upon spouses to maintain a steady emotional and moral tone felt that this should be integrated with an emotional warmth and erotic delight without which marriage would lose much of its worth. Thus they promoted the idea of an integration between spontaneity and sobriety.

This point is particularly important for those, such as myself, who are attracted to Weber's interpretation of Protestant culture, for Weber did not perceive—and, in fact, denied the existence of—the Puritan demand for integration. Weber and many later historical sociologists have taken the position that the fundamental feature of Puritanism was its ascetic, world-rejecting character; but the evidence provided by the Puritan treatment of marriage simply will not support this position. There were ascetic tendencies in Puritanism, but the Puritans also stressed constancy and self-control for a major purpose that was not ascetic. From the 1620s to the 1660s, in the great age of their writings on marriage, almost all the Puritan preachers and theologians urged spouses to maintain a steady and reliable delight in their mates, a pleasure both sensuous and spiritual. They did not call for an ascetic denial of impulse but for a fusion of self-denial and worldly desire, for a style of feeling and action which was at once self-controlled and free. A primary question of this book will be whether—or to what extent—the Puritans were successful in making this integration a psychic reality.

In this introduction I will briefly summarize the Puritan conception or elaboration of ideas of self-control, and then go on to discuss some of its consequences for the organization of relations between the sexes. In doing so, I will comment upon certain of Weber's theses which my own research has caused me to question. Before embarking on this summary, however, I would like to present and explain my somewhat unusual methodology.

There are currently a number of different approaches used in the writing of historical sociology, particularly that con-

nected with the history of the family (of marriage, childhood, and so on). Let me first describe these methods and
then locate my own procedure in relation to them.

On one side we have what might be called the study of
what actually happened: not the study of normative ideas of
how people should live or should behave or of how children
should be raised, but what parents actually did with children, what wives and husbands actually said to each other,
how they actually behaved from day to day. In some cases
this method is profitable, particularly when there are ample
source materials. In other cases the method offers little because very little is known or could be known about the real
behavior of people of a distant time and place.

At the other end of the spectrum are a variety of studies
in the history of ideas, which analyze conceptions of marriage, childhood, what a child is, what an adult is, what old
age is, what youth is, what sex is. These ideas are treated
somewhat in the manner in which people write the history
of philosophy: in terms of the influence of these ideas on
other ideas.

A third approach to the subject is the sociological history
of ideas. What was the social or economic context in which
an idea developed? How can we account for the generation
of a new or modified idea by looking at the nonintellectual
circumstances of the time?

These three methods (the study of actualities and the two
methods which adopt a history-of-ideas approach) are considered by historians to be appropriate ways of studying the
history of the family. My method is different. In part because of my training as a philosopher, I am inclined to think
about the history of culture in a way which is not always ap-
pealing to historians. My technique is to study the most
central texts of the culture under examination. These texts
have either played a major part in the development of the
culture or can be said to represent a symbolic perspective
which has played a major part.

My approach is not to ask what forces produced the text
at a particular moment in history, nor to ask whether this

was the first time the ideas presented within it ever occurred. These are both reasonable questions, but not my
question.

My interest is in seeing the text—the novel, the sermon,
the journalistic essay—as a totality, and in discovering the
ambiguities and symbolic relations between different elements of the text. Too often there is an attempt to view
ideas as having a unitary meaning. In major texts one often
finds a subtext, a hidden text which contradicts the surface
meanings. Thus it is important to employ methods of literary analysis in studying these major cultural objects.

Now, which texts can be considered major cultural objects? In my opinion, those texts or sets of texts which have
served as reference points for later periods; texts to which
people have returned, those which they have developed or
contradicted. Examples, of course, abound: the Hebrew
Scriptures, the New Testament, the major philosophical
texts of Locke, Martin Luther's translation of the Bible.
These works are important culturally not because they have
been followed to the letter or even imitated, but because
they have become sources around which later intellectuals and teachers (manipulators of cultural symbols) have
worked out new ideas. These texts are the past from which
intellectuals have made the future. And this analysis of significant texts is the method which I have used in studying
the history of conscience, marriage, and emotion in seven-
teenth- and eighteenth-century England.

One might begin to approach the Puritan elaboration of
the idea of self-control or constancy (I shall use the terms in-
terchangeably) by isolating five distinguishing characteris-
tics or elements. The first feature is a call for a steadiness of
feeling. The Puritans very much opposed the oscillating
temperament, a characteristic mode of behavior in which
emotions moved quickly back and forth, and which has
been well described in Huizinga's work on late medieval
Burgundy, *The Waning of the Middle Ages.*

In the culture of the oscillating temperament—by no
means peculiar to Burgundian culture—it was expected that

people would move abruptly from one emotion to another, from anger to fear, from joy to sadness, and that these emotions were likely to be quite extreme. This mobility of emotions was not only expected but encouraged by various social forms—for example, the ringing of bells, or the style of wandering preachers, both of which inspired an intensity of emotion on the part of the population. Behavior in the streets was tipped from friendliness to anger in a very short period and without much cause. Such phenomena are described by the late-nineteenth-century French historian Charles Petit-Dutaillis in his book on the laws of vengeance in fifteenth-century Netherlands. Petty quarrels would arise over nothing—someone would bump into someone else—and murder would result.

The oscillating temperament was encouraged by fairs, charivari, and other occasions in which unruly behavior was expected. The Puritans strenuously opposed these practices, for the same reason, I believe, that they were opposed to the theatre: not because of some intrinsic objection to the representation of life on stage, but because the theatre was a place notorious for unbridled behavior. The Puritans desired a culture which would encourage an even temperament, steadiness, and reliability. With an even temperament, one could count on oneself and on others to maintain a calm demeanor.

The idea of steadiness is not new. It is already well-developed in Stoic and in Epicurean thought, and it was represented by the behavior of Socrates at his trial and death. But the even temperament was, for the classical world, an ideal which primarily benefited the individual who possessed it and which was an ideal meant for the elite. By the time of the Puritans, it became a principle meant for everybody, men and women, cultured and uncultured, and it formed the basis of many social practices.[2]

Marcus Aurelius called for steadiness or moderation in his own feelings, but the world in which he lived and the social practices which surrounded him were not designed to encourage this mode of feeling. He might not go to the gladiatorial games, but the games existed. Similarly, Socrates, in the *Symposium*, might not get drunk, but the drinking party still existed. The Puritans, on the other hand, attempted to construct a world in which social forms would be based on the expectation and the demand for steadiness of feeling.

The second feature of this new form of self-control is a reduction in self-involvement. This can be illustrated on the most concrete level from the history of manners. Let us take, for example, talking about oneself or showing strong feelings on social occasions. Richard Steele, one of the great popular moralists of early-eighteenth-century England, says that one must exercise self-restraint in both mood and word when in company. "It is a wonderful thing," he writes, "that so many, and they not reckoned absurd, shall entertain with whom they converse by giving them the History of their Pains and Aches; and imagine such Narrations their Quota of the Conversation. This is of all other the meanest Help to Discourse; . . . Mutual good Humour is a Dress we ought to appear in wherever we meet, and we should make no Mention of what concerns our selves, without it be of Matters wherein our Friends ought to rejoyce."[3] For the same reason, intensity of emotion must be reduced, for if one is extremely excited or extremely sad, one is less aware of other people's feelings.

Della Casa and other authors of handbooks on manners in the sixteenth and seventeenth centuries put forth this normative idea of paying increased attention to others. But, as may already be apparent, a curious paradox results from this ethic: we are to be more attentive and concerned for others, but we must also, out of consideration for them, show *less* emotion. This is a third element of Puritan self-control. We should be interested in others, but not too interested. Nor should others impose their feelings upon us. The degree of attentiveness to others increases, but the degree of deep emotion which is to be shared in most sectors of life (except, as we shall see, in the most intimate sector, marriage) is to be reduced. This is the form of social life proposed and practiced by the Puritans. Its paradoxical requirements might understandably lead to charges that social life is superficial or hypocritical.

In this connection, let me relate a brief anecdote. When I was at the Institute for Advanced Study, I called up a man I had not seen for some years, a scholar at the neighboring theological school. I asked him how he was, and he said, "I'm fine." I asked him whether I was disturbing him, and he said, "Oh, no, not at all." And then in the afternoon I picked up a newspaper and discovered that this man's father, also a prominent scholar, had died the day before. But he would not let me know this; he reduced his feelings so as not to burden me. This apparent conflict or paradox is one of several brought about by the demand for constancy and self-restraint.

It should be clear that the steadiness of feeling, the reduction of self-involvement, and the restraint on open emotion are intended primarily for the benefit of others. But their consequence is a private world which may be experienced as an essential feature of oneself. Manners have played an important part in the creation of the modern individual. We know about the creation of the individual in the history of jurisprudence and in the history of economics, but here I refer to the creation of the individual as an emotional reality.

It is commonly thought that people have always possessed "interior" emotions, but this is not the case; it is a historical construction. The idea of a private, interior life is a relatively recent one. It is not found in the classical world, not even in Augustine, who is often seen as a major figure in the creation of subjectivity. One can see this development clearly, however, in the work of Addison and Steele, the English journalists who did so much to forward the development of manners in the English middle class. Writing at the beginning of the eighteenth century, they define a new idea of sociability. They call it good humor, and good humor is something which can be relied upon.

A number of Addison's and Steele's most amusing columns deal with the lives of bourgeois English gentry on summer holiday in the country. During such vacations, people tended to become bored; there was nothing to occupy them. So a certain section of the house became known as "the Infirmary," and anyone who was irritable at table—even to a servant—had to go there until he was again "fit for Society." If he went voluntarily, he received praise and special awards.[4]

It is difficult to say whether Addison and Steele were making suggestions to their readers or actually reporting on observed behaviors. At any rate, in these key texts we are presented with the idea that when one feels unpleasant emotions one must absent oneself. There is a similar description of how a widower should behave after his wife dies. He should not take part in society until he is able to recover an even temperament and good humor. The result of this new practice of keeping things to oneself was the private realm of feelings.

Today we believe a private realm is good for us; that is, of benefit to the individual. But for the Puritans and their heirs, the private realm was for the benefit of others. All sorts of new psychological problems might arise once this form of culture was in place: problems of expressivity, of being able to share feelings once one has learned to keep them in. Perhaps the popularity of therapy and psychiatry in the twentieth-century West owes something to this cultural change of two centuries ago.

A fourth feature in the Puritan conception of self-control is a new notion of the individual's capacity for constancy in both morals and emotions. I owe the development of this idea to my friend and colleague at the University of Bielefeld, Heinz-Dieter Kittsteiner, who has worked on analogous developments in orthodox Lutheranism of the seventeenth and eighteenth centuries. What Kittsteiner found for orthodox Lutheranism, and what I have found in my own work on Puritanism and its heirs, is that a new belief emerges, a belief that children can be brought up such that, as adults, they will be able to govern themselves thoroughly and constantly by their conscience. They are seen as capable of leading moral lives without notable failure.

This contrasts sharply with a fundamental conception of the Roman Catholic Church: the cycle of sin, guilt, repentance, and forgiveness built into the institution of the confession. It was expected by the Church that even the most pious people—saints, monks, nuns—would fail to fulfill, in some way or other, their moral and spiritual requirements. Confession, absolution, and penance were there to deal with these expected failures. Many Puritans also took the view that people are inevitably sinners (in their hearts, if not in their conduct); but another very strong Puritan tendency took a different attitude toward the degree of perfectability which men and women could attain in the conduct of their lives. Even among the Puritans who denied that people could be free of sin altogether, the belief was widely held that individuals were capable of governing themselves to such an extent that moral lapses of conduct, intention, and feeling could be largely avoided by anyone who had been well brought up. It was believed that any normal human being had the potential to develop this degree of self-control.

The Puritan view that people could, in fact, be thoroughly good is represented in the work of the Cambridge Platonists, an influential group of theologians associated with Cambridge University, who were highly active during the Puritan interregnum and whose students did much to form Enlightenment ideas of religion and spirituality in England. The most notable Platonists took the position that a steady experience of the presence of God was available to the ordinary person. It was not something exclusively limited to the religious virtuoso; anybody who had ethically purified his soul could know God.

This ethical purification consisted above all in a steadiness or constancy of moral temperament; that is, a thorough and secure devotion to righteousness. Purity did not mean that one could not have contrary impulses, nor did it mean that one could suffer no moral failings. Rather, the dominant and continuous feeling within oneself was a sober concern for doing good and being righteous. The Platonists thought that if a person achieved this, then God would make himself known, not just for a moment but continuously.

They therefore took a strong position against those who thought that the route to knowledge of God was through intense emotion, ecstasy, and extraordinary states of feeling. In fact, they thought that the daily life of righteousness, the development of habitual rectitude, was the key to mystical experience. The ethical purity the Platonists demanded did not require thorough rejection of the world. It did require an even temper, but this was compatible, in their view, with enjoyment of life.

The fifth and extremely significant feature of the Puritan culture of self-control is the development of its integrative or harmonious ideal. Since Nietzsche and Freud, the idea of the conscience as an enemy to mental health has certainly been well known to us. We are aware of its negative, repressive aspects. It is interesting and important to understand that the Puritans did *not* adopt an idea of conscience which involved a thoroughly ascetic attitude toward the rest of the psyche. I will argue that, although they did not want it, a repression resulted nevertheless; but, at least as an ideal, they upheld the idea of a harmonious relation between elements and were not opposed in principle to all of the pleasures of the world.

This is where I must disagree with Weber, who identified Puritanism with what he called *innerweltliche askese,* inner worldly asceticism. Here he is mistaken. The Puritans rejected the monastic life and thoroughly opposed the idea that voluntary celibacy was in any way spiritually superior to the life of the married person. The Puritans were not the first to take this attitude toward celibacy. It was a central feature of the sixteenth-century Christian humanism of More, Colet, and particularly Erasmus. The Puritans attempted to carry out the humanist opposition to the ethic of monastic asceticism in a thoroughgoing way. It is therefore surprising that Weber saw the Puritans as endorsing a monastic asceticism within the world. The Puritan's rejection of the monastic life, of celibacy as a requirement for ministerial office, and of the notion that marriage was a lower form of spiritual life than the life of the voluntary virgin who devoted him- or herself to God—all of this meant that the Puritans, in a very central area of life, upheld a life-affirming, life-accepting attitude: within the confines of the marriage bed, sexuality and sexual pleasure were not only permitted, but seen as good things. Sex was not simply for procreation or to avoid fornication but was good in itself to the degree that it gave pleasure and comfort to both husband and wife.

This facet of Puritanism may surprise the nonspecialist reader, but its existence has been noted by a number of distinguished historians and would in fact be apparent to any serious reader of seventeenth-century Puritan texts on marriage.[5] One Puritan divine, Daniel Rogers, tells us that conjugal love means "not onely Christian love, a grace of Gods spirit: (for marriage borders much what upon nature and flesh) nor yet a carnall and sudden flash of affection, corrutely enflamed by Concupiscense: (rather brutish than humane) but a sweete compounde" of both religion and nature which is "properly called *Marriage* love."[6] Richard Baxter writes that "*Husband and wife must take delight in the Love, and company, and converse of each other,*" and another theologian, Thomas Gataker, well known in his own time for his treatment of marriage, asserts that one of a husband's duties of "love" toward his wife is "*Joy & delight in her.*"[7] He continues with a passage from Proverbs, often quoted by Puritan writers on marriage: "*Drinke,* saith the wise man [of Proverbs], *the water of thine own cisterne: . . . and rejoyce in the wife of thy youth: Let her be with thee as a loving Hind, and the pleasant Roe: Let her* brests or bosome *content thee at all times: and delight continually,* or as the word there is, even *doate on the Love of her.*"[8]

This sensuous love is not simply permitted, given the existence of a higher, holier, "spiritual" relation between man and wife, to forward the other purposes of marriage. It is required as an intrinsic element of a good marriage. Sensual affection and delight must continue unabated, with the full intensity of youthful desire, throughout the whole of married life. *"Keep up your Conjugal Love in a constant heat and vigor,"* writes Richard Baxter. From the very outset, your spouse must be the apple of your eye. As life goes on, you must delight in your spouse as if he or she were your new and youthful husband or bride. You must not suffer your *"Love to grow luke-warme."*[9]

Physical deformities should not weaken your enjoyment of your spouse. If there are objectively more beautiful women or more handsome men, disadvantageous comparisons should not be made. The pleasure you take in your spouse should be so great that there should be no place for any defect.[10] Counseling the wife, Daniel Rogers says, "Poare upon your owne husband, and his parts, let him be the vaile of your eies, as *Abimelec* told *Sara,* and looke no further." Then counseling the husband, he says, let your wife "bee your furthest object: thinke you no vertues in any beyonde hers: those that are but small, yet make them great by oft contemplation: those that are greater, esteeme and value at their due rate."[11] William Gouge writes that "An husband's *affection* to his wife must be answerable to his *opinion* of her: hee ought therefore *to delight in his wife intirely; that is, so to delight in her, as wholly and only delighting in her: . . .* [I]f a man have wife, not very beautifull, or proper, but having some deformity in her body," he should nonetheless "delight in her, as if she were the fairest, and every way most compleat woman in the world."[12]

What exactly was the delight which husband and wife were supposed to take in one another? Was it a high and thoroughly excited delight, the sort associated with romantic passion and ecstasy, or was it something more sober and moderate, which we might better call enjoyment than excitement? One does not find a direct answer to this question, as far as I know, in Puritan literature, but it is safe to say from the Puritans' general concern with sobriety that they thought of this delight as a moderate feeling which did not ordinarily lead to extremes of passion.[13]

There is indirect evidence for my conviction in the attack made upon marriage in English comedy of the 1660s to the 1690s. With the reopening of the London stage upon the restoration of the monarchy and the defeat of the Puritans, a new sort of comedy was born which had as its subject courtship and marriage, and which had as its apparent aim the demonstration and elaboration of the belief that sexual excitement can be found outside of marriage—in courtship, for example—but is not something one can have for long within marriage. This theme was particularly well developed by Dryden, the founder of the genre, in a series of brilliant comedies which showed that while marriage might provide many things, it offered little stimulation and excitement. All the old hackneyed truths or half-truth—familiarity breeds boredom, the same person cannot excite someone year after year, one cannot be excited when sexual relations are a marital duty—were developed on the stage by Dryden and his colleagues. Even now we associate the theme that true sexual happiness is not to be found in marriage with Restoration comedy.

What is less well known is that there were theatrical responses to this attitude which conceded that excitement was not to be found in marriage in the long run, but which also put forward the idea that another kind of pleasure (namely, enjoyment) was available throughout married life. This point was developed by Shadwell, who replaced Dryden as poet laureate of England upon the accession of William and Mary, and who represents, I think, the underlying assumption of Puritanism about the relation between eroticism and married happiness.

There is a concession involved: the price of constancy, fidelity, and steadiness of feeling is the sacrifice of intense excitement, at least in the sexual arena and perhaps in others as well. Shadwell and other writers who promote the pleasures of enjoyment over excitement (Addison and Steele would certainly be among them) regard the trade-off as worth it. Happy and steady marriages, even if they lack excitement, are better than the temporary, albeit intense, relations that provide excitement. To others, this trade-off may not seem so satisfactory.

The Puritans called for delight within marriage, but they also called for sobriety, steadiness, and constancy— including constancy in affection, love, and erotic pleasure. This is a very tall order, and it seems apparent that the Puritans' expectations were unrealistic. They did not acknowledge how difficult it is to integrate erotic pleasure and constancy in the long term. One reason may have been their desire to make married life spiritually superior to celibacy. A more important reason is their attitude toward self-control, their belief that control of one's feelings and conduct could generally be demanded and expected of all well-brought-up people.

Up to this point I have described the normative ideal of self-control which the Puritans set forth in numerous texts. Existing letters indicate that the ideal was, in fact, practiced; but there is no substantial evidence to document the extent to which it was. I would like to conclude this introduction by examining the strain placed upon the Puritans by their attempted synthesis of carnality and conscience, and the consequences of their unrealistic expectations. To do so, I must first place the Puritans within the context of the history of gender.

The Puritans shared the general Roman Catholic attitude toward the spiritual concerns of the two sexes. Women's souls were seen as equally important as those of men; salvation was not a matter exclusively reserved for the male sex. The Puritans also maintained a certain egalitarianism with respect to the relation between man and wife in moral matters; women were expected to concern themselves with their husband's moral and spiritual state. But in all other aspects of life, the Puritans placed men and women in a clear hierarchy. Men were the heads, women were the bodies; males were to rule, females to follow. Yet along with this they called for emotional intimacy between men and women and a physical intimacy which required erotic delight on both sides.

But was an intense and passionate erotic excitement compatible with the steady and sober joy required by self-discipline and constancy? While Weber may have inaccurately viewed the Puritans as fundamentally ascetic, it is true that the ethic of mainstream Puritanism placed severe constraints upon erotic pleasure. This was not because the Puritans thought that sex was in itself bad, but because the pleasures of the erotic life are, at their fullest, highly passionate and agitated. The unintended outcome of the Puritan ethic was the prudery of Richardson's Pamela, who is dismayed by the animality of sexuality and its temporary abandonment of sobriety and self-control. The integrative ideal which the Puritans called for in marriage could not hold.

In spite of its antagonism to intense feeling and passion, the ethic of constancy had wide appeal in eighteenth-century England. It seemed to promise more stable and humane relations. But the burdens upon those who adopted it fully must have been great. Richardson's novel reveals one route that was taken to ease the burden: a hierarchy of gender developed which enabled men to avoid the psychic deficits of constancy.

In the 1740s, and even earlier, there was a new demand for prudishness on the part of women and a development of the notion that the "true" woman is not interested in sex and is more ethical than men. Women became the bearers of civilization and of moral culture and men the bearers of energy, vitality, and sexuality.

This is truly a remarkable development in light of the fact that late medieval high culture—as much a creation of men as eighteenth-century culture, if not more so—held to the classical and early medieval idea that women were the lustier of the two sexes, and that men were the bearers of culture and morality. Men attended universities, not women; women were, in fact, seen as a great threat to men, sexually speaking. By the eighteenth century a reversal occurred:

women were considered pure and without a strong sexual impulse, and although they were still excluded from morally authoritative public institutions, such as universities, morality was seen as the center of their being. How did this idea come about? How did the prudishness of the late-eighteenth and nineteenth centuries, commonly called Puritanism, develop from the nonprudish character of seventeenth-century Puritans? I can offer a few explanations, but let me first make some prefatory remarks about contemporary historians' treatment of gender.

There are currently two major conceptions of the history of ideas of male and female. One is that these ideas were developed by a ruling class to serve its own interests. The ruling class can be taken to mean men, or a certain economic class, or any group which causes women to perform tasks of one sort or another for the interests of that group, and which formulate particular ideas about woman's nature. This is a modification of a standard view of the history of morals which goes back to Thrasymachus in *The Republic* and which was elaborated by Marx: What is called moral is an expression of the interests of the stronger.

The second view is that, even though women were considered weaker, they had a hand in developing concepts of gender; the conception of woman served women's own interests, was developed by women for women, and answered the needs of women as well as men, the class that ruled the economy.

Both of these conceptions have a certain value, and I would not deny their usefulness from time to time, but in terms of the history of moral culture, they do not tell the whole story.

In that history, tasks are allotted differentially. Groups are given the task of forwarding a certain element of civilization, and anyone who has as his task the development of some aspect of culture must pay a certain price. In the eighteenth century women were given the task of carrying out the newly powerful culture of self-control. They were seen as primarily responsible for the advancement of this culture and therefore had to be truly pure in conduct and in feeling. Men were also to achieve some degree of moral development, but they were allowed to be more lusty, to fail more often: they were, after all, men. Here was the double standard. We might ask why women were given the task of self-control. Why was it not allocated in a more equitable manner? I would propose two answers. The first, which I have referred to, is the more obvious; it was convenient for men not to have to be so good. After all, this new notion of self-control had great costs. It is not easy to live the good life, the life of constancy, and it is not altogether pleasant. It was obviously to the advantage of men to leniently apply the standards of self-control to themselves, yet still be able to feel that they were vigorous supporters of self-control because they demanded so much of women. They upheld the standard but were not compelled to live by it. The division of labor (or of gender) answered men's interests and also enabled the culture (both men and women) to express a fundamental ambivalence about the value of moral purity.

Another example of this ambivalence can be found in the medieval period, where there was a strong opposition between monk and prince. The true monk lived a life of religious purity, whereas the prince lived in the world. The ambivalence has to do with the relative worth of these two kinds of lives: the monk is better than the prince, but the prince can also be seen as superior. This ambiguity is evident in a variety of medieval texts and religious documents; certain illustrations celebrate the wealthy, extravagant life of the court, but somewhere in the picture can be found a pious monk whose spiritual life is also presented as an ideal. Both ideas, that the life of the world is good and that the life away from the world is good, are retained, and a different social order elaborates each idea. The contradiction is avoided by giving one ideal, one philosophical notion, to the elaboration of one class of people and another notion to the elaboration of another class. In this way, the opposition between the two ideals is retained but made less obvious.

The same thing occurs with men and women in the eighteenth century. There is the belief that purity and self-control are best, but also doubts about the worth or truth of this belief. After all, purity leads to a life which is less enjoyable. So the conflicting ideas are given to different classes of people, in a structure which might be referred to as a reciprocal hierarchy. Women represent one idea, men the other. This elaboration allows both men and women to share in both beliefs. Women who are pure can be admired by men, and men who are lusty can be admired by women; if they cannot be pure (or lusty) themselves, they can admire another class that is. The apparent contradiction is avoided, and the experience of the ambiguity is permitted by the culture.

This reciprocal hierarchy came about, it seems to me, because the Puritans called for integration without bargaining for its psychic consequences. They developed techniques for extending the power of conscience, and the consequence of this new power was a necessary demand for a reduction in sexuality. In this reasoning, I follow Freud: when you increase the power of conscience, you do not necessarily increase its rationality. The increase of moral power can have irrational consequences.

In "The Resistances to Psychoanalysis," Freud writes, as he does in many other places, that men and women are required by modern society and civilization to live psychologically beyond their means.[14] The image is an economic one, as the author means it to be, and calls up the idea that more is paid out than received, psychologically speaking. What outrages Freud is the unwillingness of society to recognize the inadequate compensation it offers people for their moral restraint. After all, it is for the sake of society that men and women restrain themselves.

What can the individual do? How can he collect from a debtor who is often unable to pay or, in any case, unwilling to acknowledge that the debt exists? The matter is made all the more complicated by the fact that the individual is also an agent of society, and to some extent takes its part—above all, in the feelings and demands of his own conscience. He therefore not only has difficulty collecting from others, but from himself.

We all know that good people do not, in general, feel better than bad people. Why do good people feel so bad? The account which Freud gives is that good people feel bad *because* they are so good. They are subject to the power of conscience; it attacks them even when they have done nothing wrong.

I believe this is what happened in Puritanism. The increased power of conscience led, in fact, to repression—even though, in the case of the Puritans, they did not call for it. In the end, there is a certain element of truth in Weber's assertion that Puritans were ascetic. They did not seek asceticism, but if asceticism of a certain order was not a normative ideal, it was, unfortunately, a psychological reality.

But this is not the end of the tale. The steady conscience was also, though not intentionally, the creator, or at least one of the creators, of a new conception of sexuality as a steady and active force in the self, just as conscience was. The Puritans sought to make themselves thoroughly ethical in conduct and intention. To the extent that they succeeded, they gave conscience the right to claim that it was the core of one's personality. How could sexual desire and interest, which had traditionally been seen as fluctuating, sometimes in flame, sometimes not, respond to this challenge? Sexuality was in danger of being made marginal to the self. A new conception of the steady presence of sexuality, I suggest, was created so sexuality could be seen as essential to oneself.

This book is an essay in philosophical history, a genre more at home in contemporary France, Italy, and Germany than in the United States and Great Britain. Its most recent eminent practitioner is Michel Foucault, who is only one of the distinguished authors who have written in this form in the twentieth century. Some are well known: Sigmund Freud, Max Weber, Walter Benjamin. Others ought to be well known: Dolf Sternberger, Bernard Groethuysen, Norbert Elias, Benjamin Nelson. There are, of course, differences in style and method among philosophical historians, and many of these differences go back to the three great nineteenth-century authors of philosophical history, Hegel, Marx, and Nietzsche, the last being the one with whom I feel the most affinity. They were united, however, in their concern to tell the ways in which conscience and morality were expressed, in the historical development of shared forms of human life in everyday manners, law, politics, economics, and religion. The ensuing chapters delve closely into the central texts of the Puritans and their heirs, guided by the same ambition to relate some of the twists and turns of morality in history.

1

The Religious Meanings
of Constancy

$\mathbf{M}$oral constancy, as it evolved within the Puritan tradition, was intended to benefit others, but it was not comprehended purely as a social necessity. Within courtship and marriage, constancy had a psychological function, and yet it was not understood purely as answering a psychological need. The Puritan ethic of constancy also had religious and even mystical meanings, as evidenced by the writings of the Cambridge Platonists, a group of Puritan scholars active from the 1630s to the 1680s, whose name derives from their association with the University of Cambridge and their interest in the Platonic mystical tradition. The Platonists continued to preach and to publish after the interregnum and well into the late seventeenth century.

The character of their mysticism is disputed. Ernst Cassirer, in his book on the Cambridge Platonists, thinks they are best understood as having upheld the contemplative ideal: "They take their standards for . . . [philosophic] knowledge from the classical Hellenic ideal; as philosophers they recognize no other good and no higher value than the pure contemplative activity, the *noēsis noēseos*. . . . They lead a life of contemplation, of learned research, and of philosophic meditation, and they never seek to push beyond this sphere."[1] In this way, he argues, they were in sharp disagreement with the Baconians, who viewed knowledge as a source of power, as a means of gaining "a practical control of reality." The Baconian philosophy, quite powerful in the scientific milieus of seventeenth-century England, emphasized "the primacy of doing over knowing, of the concrete over the abstract, of action over contemplation." Thus, Cassirer writes, "if one forms a mental picture of the intellectual atmosphere out of which the English experimental philosophy developed, . . . the inevitable opposition between it and the Cambridge School becomes manifest at once."[2]

According to Constantinos Patrides, the Platonists promoted a form of life which was both active and contemplative. While they echoed Plotinus' reiterated counsel that man should withdraw into himself, they resisted at every turn the philosopher's admonition to isolate oneself totally from the world, to "cut away everything."[3] Patrides writes: "At no time [in the Platonists' view of contemplation] is the soul 'out of nature,' swallowed up and lost in the wide womb of the Divine. Always aware of its responsibilities within the arena of this world, it utilizes the insight gained by 'ecstasy' to propel man from contemplation into action."[4]

Both Cassirer and Patrides discuss the seventeenth-century Platonists in terms of an opposition between the active and the contemplative life similar to that found in Plato's *Republic*, Aristotle's *Nichomachean Ethics*, and in Plotinus' *Enneads*, works in which it is suggested that the experience or vision of the highest and best reality can be had only in contemplation. But to suggest that the Cambridge Platonists accepted the opposition between the active and contemplative life is wrong—at least in reference to the four outstanding thinkers of the Cambridge School: Benjamin Whichcote, Henry More, Ralph Cudworth, and John Smith. For them, the calm and purity necessary for the perception of God are to be achieved by a continuous and secure thread of moral constancy which runs through all one's actions.

Cassirer's account of the relationship between contem-

plation and action in the thought of the Cambridge Platonists is derived solely from one text of John Smith's, "The
True Way or Method of Attaining to Divine Knowledge." In
this discourse, Smith describes the highest level man can
achieve in the world as one in which he is "Metaphysical
and Contemplative."[5] The phrase indicates Smith's attachment to ways of speaking and thinking that have their origins in the ancient world. The four ranks of men he describes, of which the metaphysical and contemplative man
is the highest possible in this world, is a free adaptation of
Simplicius' commentary on Epictetus.

Smith died while in his thirties, and perhaps he made
least progress of the four toward a transcendence of the opposition between contemplation and activity. Nonetheless,
Cassirer's characterization of the Platonists cannot stand—
not even for Smith. Smith uses the phrase "Metaphysical
and Contemplative man" only once in his essay, and nowhere in his description of the four types of men (nor any-
where else, for that matter) does he criticize the active life.
Moreover, he does not say that a forgetting of all things, a
loss of sense of being in this world (which would prevent
one from engaging in the life of action), is a necessary step in
the process of knowing God.

It is true that Smith says that a man of the fourth rank,
"by *Universal Love* and *Holy Affection* abstracting himself
from himself, endeavours the nearest Union with the Divine Essence that may be, . . . knitting his own centre, if he
have any, unto the centre of Divine Being,"[6] but this should
not be understood in terms of the Plotinian characterization
of the contemplative man found in chapter 9 of *Ennead* 6.
Plotinus says that the soul must forget all things: where she
is, and even who she is. Although Smith recalls this theme,
he means something quite different: what must be sacri-
ficed is all self-love and pride in one's own virtue. Smith's
rejection of this self-contentment, which is permitted to
perfected souls by Stoic and other ancient pagan philosophies, is consistent with the Christian concern with humility before God.

The union with God which Smith describes is, above all, a union with God's *will*. In his sermon "The Existence and Nature of God," Smith writes that

> we cannot enjoy God by any Externall conjunction with him: Divine fruition . . . is an *Internall Union*, whereby a Divine Spirit *informing* our Souls, derives [sends] the strength of a *Divine life* through them; . . . It is not to sit gazing upon a Deity by some thin speculations: but it is an inward feeling and sensation of this Mighty Goodness displaying it self within us, melting our fierce and furious natures . . . into an Universall complyance with it self, and wrapping up our amorous minds wholly into it self.[7]

In "The True Way," he writes:

> What are all our most sublime Speculations of the Deity, that are *not impregnated* with *true Goodness,* but insipid things that have no tast nor life in them, that do but swell like empty froath in the souls of men? They doe not feed mens souls, but only puffe them up. . . .
>
> Divine Truth is better understood, as it unfolds it self in the purity of mens hearts and lives, then in all those subtil Niceties into which curious Wits may lay it forth. And therefore our Saviour . . . [was not] so carefull to stock and enrich the World with Opinions and Notions, as with true Piety, and a Godlike pattern of purity, as the best way to thrive in all spiritual understanding. . . . He hangs all true acquaintance with Divinity upon the doing Gods will, *If any man will doe his will, he shall know of the doctrine, whether it be of God.*[8]

In other words, we know God best in doing his will. But Smith, in speaking about this, did not altogether avoid an intimation of the old opposition between contemplation and action. More, Cudworth, and Whichcote were able to do so.

More writes that the "Incitements" to the duty to *"Love one another with a pure heart, fervently* . . . are many,"* one of which is this: "Sith that the Deity it self is nothing else but a sufficient and overflowing Goodness, creating all things, and sustaining them from no other principle than the Spirit of Goodness; though we cannot act as this absolute Deity, yet we may will according to that uncreated Will, which is nothing else but pure overspreading Love."[9]

More offers another reason to love:

Shall Envy, shall Hatred, shall Lust, Ambition, Luxury, &c. Shall all these enormous Desires and Affections be cast out of the Soul by Sanctity and Purity, that she may be but a transparent piece of Ice, or a spotless fleece of Snow? Shall she become so pure, so pellucid, so christalline, so devoid of all stains, that nothing but still shadows and night may possess that inward diaphanous Purity? . . . Thus would she be . . . but a more cleanly sepulchre of a dead starved Soul. Nay, certainly all this cleansing and preparing is for something well worth that labour. The *Stoicks* themselves, that were such severe Sentencers of Passion, would retain *philanthropia. Stoicism* it self brings in, upon that deadness and privation of other Passions, that Divine motion of the Soul, which is Love or Goodwill to all Mankind. And shall Christianity be but a cold grave to the mortified Soul of man? No surely, there is a Resurrection to Life, Love and the Divinity, as well as a Death of the enormous Affections of this Mortal Body.[10]

In his treatise on the moral life, the *Enchiridion Ethicum*, More writes that the highest happiness is not to be found in contemplation, but in the moral character of one's life. In some passages of the *Nichomachean Ethics*, writes More, Aristotle "takes part with the *Intellect,* and placeth Happiness in Contemplation. But we presume to say, this can be no *moral* Happiness; since it would be confined to a few speculative Men and Philosophers, and so shut out the Bulk of mankind, who could never be partakers thereof."

The highest happiness is not to be found in intellect, but

in what More calls "the *Boniform Faculty of the Soul*," which delights in what is moral and good in one's own and others' lives and actions. This is "the most elevated and most divine Faculty of the Soul . . . For it is not above the Talent of the meanest, to love God, and his Neighbour very heartily. And if this be done with Prudence and Purity of life, it is the Completion" of our own true happiness.[11]

In a sermon preached before Parliament in 1647 and published, by Parliamentary command, in the same year, Ralph Cudworth states the point more pungently: "every true Christian" is nourished by one thing: "it is nothing but the *life of Christ* deeply rooted in his heart which is the Chymicall Elixer that he feeds upon."[12]

> [Speculative] [k]nowledge is indeed a thing farre more excellent than riches . . . or anything else in the world besides Holinesse, and the Conformity of our wills to the will of God: but yet our happiness consisteth not in it, but in a certain Divine Temper & Constitution of soul which is farre above it . . . the Harmonious agreement between our wills and Gods will.
>
> Let us really declare, that we *know Christ*, that we are his Disciples, by our *Keeping of his Commandments:* and amongst the rest, that *Commandment* especially which our Saviour Christ himself commandeth to his Disciples in a peculiar manner; *This is my commandment, that ye love one another, as I have loved you.*[13]

Speaking of theological writings, Cudworth says:

> [T]here is a *Soul*, and *Spirit* of divine Truths, that could never yet be congealed into Inke, that could never be blotted upon Paper, which by a secret traduction and conveiance, passeth from one Soul unto another; being able to dwell and lodge no where, but in a Spirituall being, in a Living thing; because it self is nothing but *Life* and *Spirit*. Neither can it, where indeed it is, expresse sufficiently in Words and Sounds, but it will best de-

clare and speak it self in Actions: . . . the *Life* of divine Truths, is better expressed in Actions than in Words, . . . Words, are nothing but the dead Resemblances, and Pictures of those Truths, which *live* and *breath* in Actions.[14]

In his aphorisms, Benjamin Whichcote expressed like views: "God expects, Man should *Do*; as He makes him capable." "He knows most, who *Does* best." "Religion *is not* . . . a Piety of particular Fancy; consisting in some pathetic Devotions, vehement Expressions, bodily Severities, affected Anomalies and Aversions from the innocent Usages of others: *but* consisteth in a profound Humility, and an universal Charity."[15]

Speaking of God, Whichcote says: "In his *natural perfections* we cannot communicate with him, because we are creatures. His natural perfections are such as these, infiniteness, eternity, omniscience, omnipotence, omnipresence, his immensity, ubiquity, &c. In these no creature can partake with him, nor by these declare him. But in his *moral perfections* we may, and ought; and 'tis religion in us to imitate God in his moral perfections."[16] As these passages evidence, the spirit of goodness and purity necessary to know God was a fusion of self-control and spontaneity, similar to the fusion called for in the Puritan theory of marriage. It was, on the one hand, a matter of will and self-regulation; but it was also a matter of heart and soul, of an intuitive and instinctive attraction toward God and his goodness. It was a temper or constitution which never left one and which showed itself in all one's actions and intentions. For the Cambridge Platonists, one need not leave the world to know God; in fact, the only way to know God was to be very much in the world, ethically speaking.

The Platonists are, thus, far from the synthesis of active and contemplative elements found in the mystical doctrine of Saint Thomas Aquinas. For Saint Thomas, the virtue of prudence or moral good sense is infused with God's grace. God helps us perceive the good and supports our delight in it. Moreover, Saint Thomas believes that *consilium*, an inspiration or extraordinary insight into how we ought to behave, an insight which supplements the workings of our judgment, is a gift of the Holy Spirit.[17] In the prudent man's life, then, God's grace is especially present.

This view, which links the life of conscience guided by charity with the presence of God's grace, is a far cry from the view of the Cambridge Platonists. For them, man can know God and be with Him only by living in His will, by living the moral life.

The Cambridge Platonists did not believe that the insight gained by "ecstasy" should be applied in everyday action, as Patrides thought, for they did not seek a contemplative or ecstatic experience of God in the first place. Whichcote calls for "the Minds Substraction from the World" as a phase of one's religious development, but he means by this no more than a temporary withdrawal from images, so that a purely intellectual conception of Deity can be achieved.[18] This was not a recommendation to give up the active life, but simply to sit and think for a while.

When Smith says that "while the Soul . . . is *full of the Body*" it cannot know God (a passage Patrides offers in support of his interpretation), he is simply saying that men and women must turn away from "terrene and earthly passions" to achieve spiritual knowledge.[19] He does not propose even a temporary withdrawal into the contemplative or ecstatic way of life, but rather a disciplining of the passions, quite compatible with the life of action.

The common view that the Platonists were an isolated group in the Puritan interregnum, altogether out of harmony with their Puritan surroundings, should be regarded with great suspicion. In the first place, there is really no evidence of their isolation. The Platonists were esteemed and popular figures at Cambridge. Cudworth's sermon of 1647, in which he outlined the major ethical and theological doctrines of the group, was well received by the law-makers. Whichcote's counsel was sought by Oliver Cromwell.

Scholars have supposed that the Platonists must have

been isolated because of their denial of the basic Calvinist tenet that God foreordains some to be saved and others to be damned; in Abraham Tuckney's letters to Whichcote, his former student, he criticises Whichcote's belief in human freedom to achieve salvation.[20] But this is hardly substantial evidence of the group's isolation. And Puritanism was a varied and complex tissue of beliefs and feelings, by no means always having this harsh doctrine as its center.

In their emphasis on knowing God through living in His will, the Platonists develop a characteristic emphasis on moral constancy. They make a steadiness in God's will the center of their religious philosophy, and are thus very much at home in the Puritan world. They offer a practical route to avoid a never-ending inner conflict which Sacvan Bercovich believes is characteristic of Puritanism. On the one hand, we are not to follow ourselves, but the Lord. The self was "the great snare," the "false Christ," a spider's web spun "out of our bowels," the very "figure or type of Hell." Yet to turn against oneself, to loathe oneself, to root out the "Devil's poison and venome or infection of Self," can be experienced as an affirmation of oneself, even if it is in an act of self-attack and is genuinely felt to be in the name and the service of the Lord. According to Bercovich, the Puritans characteristically had the sense that even in self-denial there was a dreadful self-assertion.[21] If I judge myself a sinner, who is judging? Theologians may have had a solution for the problem, Bercovich admits, but in experience, he thinks, the Puritans came closer to the words of a popular early seventeenth-century poem by George Goodwin: "Unto myself my Selfe my Selfe betray . . . I cannot live, with nor without my Selfe."[22]

The Platonists had an experiential solution to the apparently inescapable prison of selfhood. It was not the obvious theological solution affirmed by many Puritans, that not only our selves, but God and His Spirit, could act within us and guide our words and deeds. (This, Bercovich thinks, did not commonly resolve the self-conflict actually experienced by the Puritan.) The Platonists' solution was to affirm the practical and real possibility of the union of ourselves with God in the daily acts of a thoroughly realized moral life. There is no more need, then, to ask whether God or oneself is acting. It is both our own will and His will, made one through our possession of a habitual and constant moral temper.

The Puritan emphasis on moral constancy has weighty emotional consequences. Constancy is a calm virtue, requiring a judicious, sober, and reflective mood—a settled temper. The thoughtful quality demanded for moral judgment is not well sustained by intense and violent emotions. Those who believe they can come to know God through the virtue of constancy must also realize that they cannot know Him— nor the cosmos in which He breathes His presence— through a violent or intense emotion. They will not find him in the tears of loss, nor in the rage of hurt, nor in deep and continued suffering. Smith, for example, approves of the words of the Rabbi, who says that God cannot be known in moments of deep sorrow or great anger.[23]

The belief that one can live in God only through a prudent and devoted conscience is limiting, for it gives all of its energy to the moral life. All that opposes the reasonable temper, all intense, extreme, or violent feelings about oneself and others, lose their value. And, whether one wishes them to be or not, these deep and sometimes violent feelings of the soul are at the very center of one's being. As such, they deserve more esteem than the mainstream Puritan tradition granted to them.

The emphasis placed by Puritanism on moral constancy, calm, and self-controlled moods has achieved great power in Anglo-American culture; analogous views have obtained great success in other parts of the West, both Protestant and Catholic.[24] Within the world of high culture, William Blake and others speak for the opposing view—but theirs remains a weak countercurrent in the ocean of Anglo-American moral and religious thought. The knowledge of God through violent emotion persists in what are generally regarded as the less reputable Protestant denominations. (The Platonists' attitude, well established in the Church of England in the eighteenth century, caused Anglicans such as Joseph Butler to think the Methodists mad. John Wesley, in preaching to the colliers on a hill outside of Bristol, spoke so vigorously of sin, damnation, and redemption, that many of his audience went into fits in experiencing their fallen state.)[25] Elsewhere in the West, other modern proponents of violent emotion have been hostile to Christian piety: Baudelaire, Lautréamont, Nietzsche, and the French Surrealists come to mind, but their views must still be regarded as minority opinions.

In the world of Dostoyevsky and other Russian writers of the nineteenth and twentieth centuries, moral truth and spiritual knowledge are achieved through intense and even violent feeling and suffering. This attitude continues to govern an important element of the Russian intelligentsia today. It accounts for what may seem otherwise peculiar comments by Aleksandr Solzhenitsyn at the Harvard commencement of 1978, when he complained of the lack of depth and developed character in the American personality.[26] From the Russian perspective, the sober ethicality of many Americans, and their discomfort in the face of intense and violent feeling, may make them appear pale and thin characters indeed.[27] The ethic of constancy put forth by the Cambridge Platonists, which brought with it a new demand for sober and judicious behavior (in essence, a new notion of conscience), had certain distinct drawbacks—foremost was that levels of affect, of feeling, had to be concomitantly reduced. Thus, the cultural and spiritual demand was a psychic demand as well.

What were the benefits for those who practiced the ethic? Although ecstasy had no place in the Puritans' religious experience, their religious and ethical constancy had an important transcendent aspect. Through one's moral purity, it was felt, the presence of the divine would be infused in all the daily acts of life. The Platonists thus provided the Puritan with practical means by which he could realize what Perry Miller has called "the Augustinian strain" at the heart of

Puritan piety: "the desire to transcend his imperfect self, to open channels for the influx of energy which pervades the world, but with which he himself is inadequately supplied." It was not the eternal presence of sin which Miller says was central to the Puritan experience, but the hope and search for a means by which the beauty of God could be "carried across the gulf of separation" to become inwardly present to each of us.[28] In this respect, the Platonists were thoroughly "Augustinian" in their piety. But their way contrasts quite sharply with the popularly held images of the Puritan stretched on the rack of sin and ever conscious of how much his humanity separates him from the presence of God. Here are a group of theologians—impeccably Puritan in their credentials—who offer a continuous and sweet experience of God as a real and practical possibility. Our sinfulness is not so great that God will refuse us if we live in the temper which welcomes Him. Many think of the Puritan tradition as a source of the divided soul, at war with itself. There was indeed a strain in Puritanism that was like this, and perhaps we know it best because it was the most dramatic form of the Puritan inner life. But there was another calmer and happier tendency which the Platonists reveal, which was extraordinarily influential in the creation of the middle-class culture of late-seventeenth- and eighteenth-century England. The ethic of constancy was at the core of this more generous vision of human possibilities.

Was the presence of God recompense for the costs of the ethic of constancy? Were the Puritans and those who followed them in the ethic truly equipped to carry it out or, more significantly, to cope with its consequences? We shall encounter these same questions as we investigate the impact of the ethic of constancy on other realms of the Puritan tradition.

2

The Political Meanings
of Constancy

The political meaning of the demand for moral constancy was inherently neither egalitarian nor hierarchical. This can best be seen by tracing the development of theories of child-raising from the Puritans to perhaps their most important heir, John Locke.

In the case of the Puritans, the moral self-control instilled in children was not seen as preparation for a world of adults who met as equals. Hierarchy was as much a feature of the Puritan's social world as it was of his relation to God, and in seventeenth-century England, any relation of superiority and subordination was thought to be like that of parent and child. The religious teaching of the Church of England,

> extending without interruption at least from the reign of Edward VI, consisted of a social and political inter-pretation of the duty to obey parents enjoined by the Decalogue; the simple requirement to "Honour thy fa-ther and mother" was expanded to include loyalty and obedience to the king of all magistrates, as well as to masters, teachers, and ministers. This reading of the Fifth Commandment appeared in . . . the catechism, which *everyone* had to learn.[1]

Children in New England were by no means exempt: "Puritan children, studying the famous catechism prepared by John Cotton, learned to answer the question 'Who are here [in the fifth commandment] meant by Father and Mother?' with the words, 'All our Superiors, whether in Family, School, Church, and Common-wealth.'"[2]

Of course, those who used the Fifth Commandment in this way were not required to suppose that the duties and rights of magistrate, clergyman, or landlord, were in all respects like that of a father and mother to their children; each office could be understood to have its distinct duties and privileges.[3] What all superiors had in common was that they were set over their inferiors by God's will and law, as parents were set over children by His law. Superiors deserved "Revereance and Obediance, Service and Maintenance, Love and Honour," just as parents did.[4]

The family was thus seen as the natural and appropriate place to prepare children to take part in larger social realities; for the relationship of parent to child within the family was like all relationships the child would encounter throughout his life. It was simply the first such relation. William Gouge wrote that "a family is a little Church, and a little common-wealth, at least a lively representation thereof, whereby tryall may be made of such as are fit for any place of authority, or of subjection in Church or common-wealth. Or rather it is as a schoole wherein the first principles & grounds of government & subjection are learned: whereby men are fitted to greater matters in Church or common-wealth."[5]

This use of the relationship between parents and children had support from the Stuart kings, for they believed it would reinforce their own claim to the loyalty of their subjects. The Stuart kings were not alone in thinking that a willingness to submit to parental power was the best preparation for obedience to a strong monarch. In 1639, a French royal declaration stated that "the natural respect of children towards their parents is the bond of the legitimate obedience of subjects towards their sovereigns."[6]

Paternal power was particularly favored by the "new Renaissance State" in France and England. The Stuart and Bourbon kings sought to centralize their power and to direct all political loyalty to the throne; they were thus firm opponents of loyalties to cousins and distant kin, especially among the aristocracy. Such networks of allegiance were "a direct threat to the states' own claim to prior loyalty."[7] But a stress on the subordination of children to their own father within the immediate family was no such threat; indeed it was seen as a basis for a firm and unswerving obedience to the sole and absolute rule of the monarch. "The State was as supportive of the patriarchal nuclear family as it was hostile" to the family oriented to kin.[8]

John Locke, some decades later, sees the political meaning of a capacity for moral self-regulation as different from what the Puritans saw, but his new attitude reflects a concern for moral constancy which the Puritans themselves promoted. For Locke, the development of a moral self-control in childhood was preparation for the freedom and independence which comes with adulthood.

Although Locke remained a bachelor throughout his life, he had much experience in raising and educating children. From 1660 to 1666, as part of his duties as lecturer in Greek at Christ Church, Oxford, he had several students under his tuition. His tutorial duties, writes James Axtell, "consisted primarily of ministering to the intellectual and domestic needs of up to ten pupils ranging in age from thirteen to eighteen."[9] He was truly in loco parentis; his account book indicates that on one pupil's behalf he spent money for "door keys, paper, laundry, bedmaker, butler, caution money, nurses, doctors and medicine for illnesses, and tutor's fees."[10]

Locke's interest and studies in medicine led to his meeting Anthony Ashley Cooper, Lord Ashley (later the first Earl of Shaftesbury) in 1666. Ashley took a liking to Locke and that year invited him to London to be his medical advisor and general aide. At Exeter House, the London home of Lord Ashley, Locke took on both pediatric and pedagogical duties. He was given full educational and medical charge of Ashley's fifteen-year old son and sole heir, who was sickly. After the son's marriage (in a match arranged by Locke himself), he supervised, from near or afar, the education and general upbringing of the seven children of this marriage. The eldest son and heir (later to become the third Earl of Shaftesbury, a philosophical luminary of late-seventeenth-century England), was put under Locke's particular charge. Shaftesbury wrote that Locke had "the absolute direction of my education." Locke did more than direct the third Earl's education; in his capacity as household physician, he even assisted at his birth.[11]

After the first Earl of Shaftesbury lost his government offices in 1675, Locke left Exeter House and voyaged in France. Through letters, he continued to concern himself with the education of the Shaftesbury family. After a year and a half in France, he undertook, at the behest of the elder Shaftesbury and his friend Sir John Banks, the direct care of Banks's son Caleb on a tour "to let him see the manners" of the French. When this grand tour ended in 1679, Locke never again had children or young men under his personal supervision, but by this time, as Axtell puts it, he "had passed through a whole spectrum of gentlemanly educational experience—Oxford don, pediatrician, private tutor, and travelling governor on the grand tour."[12]

In the mainstream Puritan tradition, the submission of a child to his parents was an essential element in the development of moral self-control. This is the main idea of Locke's *Some Thoughts Concerning Education*, based on a set of letters which he wrote to Edward Clarke in 1684 and 1685, in answer to Clarke's request for counsel on the education of his son Edward, Jr. A successful resolution of the natural struggle between parent and child which establishes the full authority of the parents can also help resolve the struggle between reason and willfulness within the growing child.[13] The acknowledgment of parental authority can strengthen the internal authority of the child's own reason.

The struggle between parents and child begins early,

Locke says, for a child loves *"Dominion"* even more than he loves "Liberty. . . . And this is the first Original of most vicious Habits, that are ordinary and natural. This love of *Power* and Dominion shews itself very early, . . . Children as soon almost as they are born . . . cry, grow peevish, sullen, and out of humour, for nothing but to have their *Wills.* They would have their Desires submitted to by others." This love of dominion leads a child to contend with his parents "for Mastery"; the parents must win, for if they do not, they will not only end up his slave, but make him a slave to his own willfulness. "[W]hen their Children are grown up," parents, who did not take their children in hand when young, "complain, that the Brats are untoward and perverse." They should not be surprised; since their children had their way over parents and tutors when young, why should they not continue to be willful when older?[14] But if parental mastery is achieved in the name and spirit of reason, the child will become an adult who turns to his own reason for guidance in matters of conduct and belief. The rigorous rule of a young child is justified because it trains him to rule himself as an adult.

The willfulness which is expressed in children's desire to have their way has an opponent within their own souls: their own good judgment, which has, however, little power at first. Locke does not believe that a power sufficient to command conduct will develop in the child without help from adults. Rationality does attract children, for the growth of their rational capacities is a sign to them of their maturity.

"[I]f I mis-observe not," Locke writes, "they love to be treated as Rational Creatures sooner than is imagined" (*Thoughts*, sec. 81). Locke grants that a child's attraction to the use of reason is not based solely on parental demand and example. In some way (he does not make clear how) children come to realize that the use of reason is an essential element of maturity, whether or not their parents make much use of it. But the child's natural respect for rationality as an element of maturity conflicts with his observation that grown-ups are free to do whatever they want, reasonable or not. Parents must conduct themselves in the name and spirit of reason if they wish moral and rational self-control to be the uppermost ambition of their child.

Two senses of rationality must be distinguished to understand what Locke means when he says that even young children can perceive the rationality of many adult actions. An act is rational *in spirit* if it is guided by considerations genuinely thought to be reasonable by the agent; it is *substantively* rational if it is truly appropriate when judged from a rational point of view. Locke believes that very young children can often tell when their parents' conduct toward them is rational in spirit, even if they cannot judge its substantive rationality. Addressing parents, he explains that when he says that children "must be *treated as Rational Creatures*," he means that "you should make them sensible by the Mildness of your Carriage, and the Composure even in your Correction of them, that what you do is reasonable in you, and useful and necessary for them: And that it is not out of *Caprichio,* Passion or Fancy, that you command or forbid them any Thing. This they are capable of understanding" (*Thoughts,* sec. 81).

But children's attraction to their own rationality is a weak force in comparison to other desires, above all their desire to have their own way. Children cannot tame themselves; therefore, parents must tame their children for them. Children must submit to the reason of the parents: "He that is not used to submit his Will to the Reason of others, *when* he is *Young,* will scarce hearken to submit to his own Reason when he is of an Age to make use of it" (*Thoughts,* sec. 36).

Given all this, it is no wonder that Locke tells us that the true secret of education is to maintain "a Child's Spirit, easy, active and free," while instilling a habit of submission to parental authority and rational standards (*Thoughts,* sec. 46). By *spirit,* Locke means will, energy, assertiveness, and force of character. Without it, one is of as little use to oneself as to one's friends.

"If the *Mind* be curbed, and *humbled* too much in Children; if their *Spirits* be abased and *broken* too much, by too strict an Hand over them, they lose all their Vigor and Industry, and are in a worse State" than those children who have no mastery over their inclinations. "For extravagant young Fellows, that have Liveliness and Spirit, come sometimes to be set right, and to make Able and Great Men; But *dejected Minds*, timorous and tame, and *low Spirits*, are hardly even to be raised, and very seldom attain to any thing" (*Thoughts*, sec. 46).

The most dangerous emotions between parent and child, says Locke, are those of the parents. Parents must display a cool and thoughtful spirit to their children, and not an impulsive outpouring of anger or affection. "[F]requent, and especially passionate *Chiding*," Locke writes, is of "ill consequence. It lessens the Authority of the Parents, and the Respect of the Child: For . . . they distinguish early betwixt Passion and Reason: And as they cannot but have a Reverence for what comes from the latter, so they quickly grow into a contempt of the former; . . . natural Inclination will easily learn to slight such Scare-crows, which make noise, but are not animated by Reason" (*Thoughts*, sec. 77).

Locke believes that parents naturally love their children, which is one of the reasons why they concern themselves with their sons' and daughters' intellectual education. As long as this love expresses itself through a moral concern for the child's character, no problem arises, but when the love occurs in an unmediated form as open affection, there is much danger. "Parents, being wisely ordain'd by Nature to love their Children, are very apt, if Reason not watch that natural affection very warily, are apt, I say, to let it run into Fondness. They love their little ones, and 'tis their Duty: But they often, with them, cherish their Faults too" (*Thoughts*, sec. 34).

What are the moral faults which parents cherish when love of their children runs into fondness? Ultimately, they all become one fault, the fault of unrestrained self-assertion. Children "must not be crossed, forsooth; they must be permitted to have their Wills in all things; . . . The Fondling must be taught to strike, and call Names; must have what he Cries for, and do what he pleases. Thus Parents, by humoring and cockering them when *little*, corrupt the Principles of Nature in their Children" (*Thoughts*, secs. 34–35).

Parental delight in the assertiveness of their children is the stuff of disaster. Fond parents breed willful children—and ultimately willful adults—who will never respect others or care for themselves, as reason requires. This coddling is as unfortunate on the physical level as it is on the moral; Locke warns mothers that "most Children's Constitutions are either spoiled, or at least harmed, by *Cockering and Tenderness*" (*Thoughts*, sec. 4).

Parents should let their children know that they take no delight in self-assertion: "The first thing they should learn to know should be, that they were not to have any thing, because it pleased them, but because it was thought fit for them." They should thus never be "suffered to have what they once cried for" (*Thoughts*, sec. 38).

In his conception of the emotional relations between parents and children, Locke recapitulates and extends Puritan notions of child-raising, which do not come out of the same attitude toward spontaneous feelings of love and delight which informs Puritan notions of marriage.[15] In marriage, the Puritans saw it as possible to join constancy and open affection, but they denied this possibility in the case of parent-child relations. Rationally speaking, there is no more reason to distrust spontaneity and warmth in the one case than in the other; the contradictory attitudes reveal an ambivalence toward spontaneous affections. These are said to be dangerous because they threaten a loss of the capacity for self-control, not in oneself but in one's child. But the fear of a child's response to open affection may be simply a disguised concern for one's own steadiness and self-mastery and the effect upon them of strong feelings.

Just as the Puritan theory of marriage demanded that the elements of delight and love between spouses be made constant, so Locke demands that a restrained, stern, and somewhat suspicious attitude be the steady temper of parents. He thus places a hostile element at the center of the parental temper, believing that it will serve the child's own growth toward moral constancy. The theories of marriage and of child-raising both reject the idea that each pole of an ambivalence should receive some free elaboration; a thorough constancy in feeling and intention is preferred.

Locke acknowledges that the severity of his method potentially endangers the child, but he makes no acknowledgment of its danger to parents. The requirement that parents thoroughly restrain their expression of affection toward their children undoubtedly costs parents dearly. Perhaps Locke believes parents can survive this inhibition, comforted by the conviction that they are serving the moral well-being of their child; this belief would be in line with the general Puritan attitude about child-raising. On the other hand, he may perceive substantially more benefits than costs to parents who maintain a cool sobriety toward their children; their own steadiness is protected by their sobriety.

By his methods, Locke says, children will gain "an ingenuous Education" (Thoughts, sec. 45)—an education on the one hand designed to bring up a child "noble in . . . character . . . generous . . . high-minded"; and on the other hand an "education befitting a free-born person" or "one of honourable station." Today one would say that Locke's object is a liberal education.[16]

The two distinct senses of ingenuous raise problems, however. Was Locke's method of education suited to those meant for servile positions? Might not a reliance on their own judgment of what is permitted by law, civil or moral, make their lives miserable—if they survived at all? Should day laborers, wholly dependent upon the economic goodwill of others, speak and act their mind as gentlemen do? Should servants who live in the family, and who are considered to be under the paternal authority of the master of the house, have this self-reliance? Should women, even gentlewomen, govern themselves as gentlemen do? Is Locke's method really suited or meant for all children?

The same questions can be raised in light of the unequal distribution of political rights in late-seventeenth-century England. Locke is no democrat; he does not advocate the extension of suffrage to poor men or to any women. Can we suppose that he nonetheless believes all should be educated to act according to their own judgment of what law requires? Why would Locke believe this education is suited to all if he also thinks most people must rest content to be ruled by others in politics, marriage, and work?

Such questions might lead us to conclude that Locke's system of moral education was meant only for the sons of gentlemen. As adults, they could make good use of a self-reliant attitude in moral and legal matters. Politics would be open to them. They would be nobody's servant or wife, and their economic well-being would free them from having to act in a servile manner in order to make a living. This conclusion is reinforced by Locke's own statements concerning the purpose of *Thoughts*.

He introduces the book by saying that it is aimed at "our English *Gentry*," for he is concerned *"that young Gentlemen should be put into (that which everyone ought to be sollicitous about) the best way of being formed and instructed."* If those of the rank of gentlemen *"are by their Education once set right, they will quickly bring all the rest into Order."* He concludes the book by saying that he desires only to present "some general Views, in reference to the main End, and aims in Education, and those designed for a Gentleman's Son."[17]

I would nonetheless argue that Locke believes his method of moral education is fit for all. His statement of purpose is made with reference to the whole book, and he does not necessarily believe that only gentlemen can benefit from the methods described therein; some methods are particularly suited to gentlemen or their betters, but the fundamental elements of moral training have wider application.

Young gentlemen require "breeding"; that is, they must be taught the carriage and manners which will prepare them to act and feel in a manner suitable to their station. They should not be taught the manners suitable to a prince or nobleman; nor should they have the breeding of someone of lower station. Gentlemen are in the middle of the social hierarchy; they must know how to conduct themselves with appropriate dignity in the presence of their equals, their inferiors, and their superiors.[18]

A gentleman's education must address the leisure he will have as an adult; thus his tutors should introduce him to science, mathematics, philosophy, and other subjects which he may choose to pursue more deeply as an adult. His leisure will also permit him to take a responsible part in public life; to do so is his proper calling (*Thoughts*, sec. 94). Hence a gentleman's child must learn history, law, and political theory and have sufficient experience in political life (when he is old enough to gain it) in order to play an intelligent part in the public world.[19] In his private affairs, a gentleman may be faced with substantial matters of business, investment, and finance; therefore he must be prepared step by step for these things as well. It is more important for a son to learn to "manage his Affairs wisely" than to learn Greek and Latin.[20]

All these things should be taught to those who will be gentlemen, but the chief object of education, the creation of a virtuous character which includes moral self-reliance, is not reserved for gentlemen, noblemen, or princes. This object should guide the education of anyone, high or low, male or female. Reflecting on the education of a son, Locke writes, "I place *Vertue* as the first and most necessary of those Endowments, that belong to a *Man* or a Gentleman; . . . Without that I think, He will be happy neither in this, nor in the other World" (*Thoughts*, sec. 135, second italics mine).

Women deserve no less. Locke writes that "the principal aim" of his discourse is "how a young Gentleman should be brought up from his Infancy, which, in all things will not so perfectly suit the Education of *Daughters;* though where the Difference of Sex requires different Treatment, 'twill be no hard Matter to distinguish" (*Thoughts,* sec. 6). At one point in the correspondence, Mrs. Clarke requested Locke to counsel her on the education of their daughter Elizabeth. In his response, Locke wrote, "Since . . . I acknowledge no difference of sex in your mind relating . . . to truth, virtue and obedience, I think well to have no thing altered in it from what is [writ for the son]."[21] In illustration of his thesis that parents must not brook obstinacy on the part of their children, Locke praises the *mother* who was "forced to whip her little *Daughter,* at her first coming home from Nurse, eight times successively the same Morning, before she could master her *Stubbornness* and obtain a compliance in a very easie and indifferent matter" (*Thoughts,* sec. 78, first italics mine).

Locke's theory of moral education has strong political implications for both men and women, as revealed in his *Two Treatises of Government.* In the second treatise, Locke writes that "all *Parents*" are, "by the Law of Nature, . . . *under an obligation to preserve, nourish, and educate*" their Children, who are "the Workmanship" of God. He defines parental responsibility in matters of education in these broad terms: parents must give "such vigour and rectictude" to their children's minds as will make them "most useful to themselves and others" as adults. More specifically, they must prepare their children for the freedom to which they have a right as adults. For while children are not born in freedom, they are "born to it." Young children are in want of judgment, and thus need restraint and discipline; parents therefore have a right to govern them. But a child ends his nonage when he comes to the use of his reason. This permits him to know "the Law of Reason" which should govern all his acts. His own understanding of this common law of nature gives him the right to rule his own will.[22]

If a child lives "under the positive Laws of an Establish'd Government," he has the capacity to know these laws and to rule his will in accordance with them. He has a liberty,

equal to his father's, "to dispose of his Actions and Posses-
sions according to his own Will, within the Permission of
that Law." Moreover, he has the ability to ascertain whether
the government and its laws conform to the higher law of
reason which defines and limits the purposes and powers of
civil government; government has a rightful claim to his
obedience only if it does so. As an adult, he should evaluate
his government and its rulers in the light of this higher law;
in this, as in all other matters, he should govern his will by
his own understanding.[23]

Parents must educate their child so that when he is
grown, he shall see none of his superiors as fathers or mothers to whom he owes the obedience he owed his parents
when he was young. Locke does not allow the relation between parents and children to be a model for relations outside the family.[24]

Locke rejects the view that the family is a microcosm of
the larger social world. The attitude young children should
have toward their parents is not the attitude they should
have as adults to political or other superiors. The powers of
kings, or of any magistrates of the civil order, are not forms
of parental power. Locke rejects Filmer's claim that kings
have a right to command the obedience of their subjects because they are the proper heirs to the paternal power which
Adam had over his children.[25] The right which "Parents
have by Nature, and which is confirmed to them by the *5th*
Commandment, cannot be . . . political Dominion," Locke
says, for it "contains nothing of the Magistrates Power in
it."[26]

Children must begin their moral growth with a firm and
ultimate allegiance to their own parents. Loyalty to an ab-
straction cannot yet take place, and at first parents should
not seek to distinguish the authority of reason from the
authority of their own persons. But if parents embody the
spirit of rationality in their own acts and speech, in time the
child will see the law of reason as a separate object of deep
devotion.

This evolution should not, however, take place in civil society, according to Locke. The powers of a magistrate should never be seen as residing in his very person, for law, either natural or civil, is the sole source of the legitimate powers of any element of civil government. Subjects should understand civil authority in this way. The allegiance they give to the executor of the laws established by their legislature should be "nothing but an Obedience according to Law." They should be careful to distinguish the executor's person from the laws themselves; their loyalty must be to the latter, which leads them to obey the executor. If the executor violates the law, "he has no right to Obedience, nor can claim it otherwise than as the publick Person vested with the Power of the Law, and so is to be consider'd as the Image, Phantom, or Representative of the Commonwealth, . . . declared in its Laws; and thus he has no Will, no Power, but that of the law" (*Treatises*, II, sec. 151).

The executor of the laws has power by virtue of the laws of the commonwealth, and the laws must be made by legislators who act on its behalf. Members of the commonwealth should no more give their ultimate allegiance to these legislators than they should to the executor of the laws, for legislators can lose their legitimacy as well. They do so when they go against the rational purpose of a legislature, which is to protect the rights and liberties of all subjects. Therefore, people must make a sharp distinction between the persons of the legislators and the rational purposes which may justify their rule:

> [T]he Legislative being only a Fiduciary Power to act for certain ends, there remains still *in the People a Supream Power* to remove or *alter the Legislative*, when they find the *Legislative* act contrary to the trust reposed in them. . . . [T]hus the *Community* perpetually *retains a Supream Power* of saving themselves from the attempts and designs of any Body, even of their Legislators, whenever they should be so foolish,

and so wicked, as to lay and carry on designs against the Liberties and Properties of the Subject. (*Treatises,* II, sec. 149)

A parent may rightfully govern the will of his young children without their consent; the law of nature or reason gives this power to parents "for the Benefit of their Children during their Minority, to supply their want of Ability, and understanding how to manage" themselves. But "*Voluntary Agreement*" alone "*gives . . . Political Power to Governours.*" In the ordinary course of affairs, consent to their rule is given implicitly by the use of freedoms which they sustain; for example, by ownership of land which they protect, or even by use of the roads of the commonwealth.[27] But this consent may properly be withdrawn when the governors no longer rule in accord with the law, civil or natural, which sustains their authority.

Children must give their ultimate allegiance to their parents, for children have inadequate knowledge of the laws by which they should govern themselves. Adults, on the other hand, must give their ultimate allegiance to no other person; they must not find other "mothers" and "fathers." Their knowledge of law alone should command their obedience to civil authorities.

Locke's demand for universal moral autonomy had implications for marriage as well as for politics proper. Locke, like Puritan and other seventeenth-century writers on marriage, believed that an agreement to marry had the character of a contract.[28] He differed from these writers in thinking that spouses themselves should, in principle, have a great deal of latitude in setting the terms of the contract. Their freedom should not be unlimited, for marriage has natural purposes, and spouses may not set terms which would impede the achievement of those purposes. Marriage's chief purpose is "the continuation of the Species," an end not fulfilled simply by procreation; it requires that the young be nourished and supported "till they are able to shift and provide for themselves. . . . Inheritance," too, must be "taken care for"

(*Treatises*, II, secs. 79, 81). A man and woman who have taken on this purpose by marrying must therefore remain together until all this is accomplished.

Locke also says that parental care and support is a right of children; once created, a child has a rightful claim to aid from his parents. Inheritance is another natural right of children, who thus have a claim against their parents even as adults.[29] The rights of children also require that husband and wife stay together. But for how long? Locke sees no inherent reason why the marriage compact "may not be made determinable," or of limited duration, to end "either by consent, or at a certain time, or upon certain Conditions"—that is, when children can stand on their own two feet and when their inheritance is taken care of. Marriage would then be like other "voluntary Compacts," which need not be made for life. There is no necessity in the nature of marriage, "nor to the ends of it, that it should always be for Life."[30] Indeed, beyond the natural purposes of marriage which bind the partners to certain terms, the ends of marriage should be set by the partners themselves; the terms of a marriage contract should answer the particular interests of those who wed.

Laslett notes that Locke was prepared to go even farther than this. In his *Diary*, Locke made notes for the rules of a society based on reason alone, which he named Atlantis. In this society, "He that is already married may marry another woman with his left hand. . . . The ties, duration and conditions of the left hand marriage shall be no other than what is expressed in the contract of marriage between the parties."[31] Perhaps Locke thinks that since the business of procreation is taken care of by the husband's first marriage, then the parties to the second wedding are free to design their marriage as they wish.

Locke's fundamental conceptions of marriage and education are thus built upon the notion that both men and women are autonomous beings. The hierarchy between parent and child is not a model for the relation between man and wife. In spite of this belief, Locke says that husbands should have the final say in marital disputes over things held in common, for the final decision must be made by someone and "it naturally falls to the Man's share, as the abler and the stronger" (*Treatises*, II, sec. 82). As in the political arena, Locke drew back from the full implications of his egalitarian views.[32]

Why did he do so? Between autonomous equals, it is not necessary that the right to make the final decision in cases of dispute be placed always in the same party. In some cases, as with contracts generally, it can be left to a neutral third party, such as an arbitrator or a judge. In other cases, where a dispute is to remain within the family, understandings can be reached about who is to decide in particular cases or areas. Or there can be an agreement to delay the decision, if possible, until accord can be reached. Locke was surely familiar with all of these routes. Therefore, his belief that it is "necessary, that the last Determination, *i.e.* the Rule, should be placed somewhere" (*Treatises*, II, sec. 82), and that the rule naturally falls to the man, requires explanation.

Was Locke afraid of being openly radical about marriage? Being outspoken in this matter might not have helped the political purposes of the *Two Treatises*. Perhaps Locke was subject to the burdens of conscience created by the Puritan demand for constancy, which led to a desire for a hierarchy which would reduce the psychic cost to men. On the manifest or consciously logical level, a capacity for thorough moral self-regulation in both husband and wife would naturally justify their autonomy and equality, since they could generally be relied upon to act in morally responsible ways toward one another. It would also justify a mode of settling disputes which did not give all authority to the male. On the unconscious level, however, superiority may have been perceived as a form of compensation for the moral burdens imposed by an ever-vigilant and ever-powerful conscience.

The reality of this particular mode of psychic regulation became clearer as the Puritan tradition of self-regulation grew in strength and popularity in the eighteenth century.

3

The Social Purposes
of Constancy

Who benefits from the creation of a constant temper? Is it of direct benefit to the individual or does it primarily benefit others? The ancient Stoics saw it as answering the interests of its possessor, above all because his equanimity is not easily dislodged by what happens to him. He remains unperturbed, emotionally independent from his circumstances. Marcus Aurelius and Seneca hoped to triumph over the vicissitudes and alterations of life by maintaining a constant temper in the face of a changing world.

In contrast to this attitude is the oscillating temperament, a socially accepted mode of being which has had a long history in the West. Huizinga's great book on the culture and emotional life of fifteenth-century Burgundy describes it well. "All things," he writes, "presenting themselves to the mind in violent contrasts and impressive forms, lent a tone of excitement and passion to everyday life and tended to produce . . . [a] perpetual oscillation between despair and distracted joy, between cruelty and pious tenderness."[1]

This oscillation of feeling was held to be legitimate by at least some of those who held positions of leadership or respect. A town's church bells would ring out, first gloomy bells then lively bells, first bells of despair then bells of hope. The ringing, says Huizinga, must at times have been extraordinarily intoxicating. Processions were "a continual source of pious agitation." "Public mourning still presented the outward appearance of a general calamity"—and people responded to it as such. "The sermons of itinerant preachers," who came "to shake the people by their eloquence," were another source of agitation.[2] Executions and other judicial punishments excited many and apparently were meant to do so. The very character of public life in the Burgundian realm was imbued with the belief that such oscillations of feelings were right and proper, to be participated in by the people and encouraged by those in authority.

Huizinga thinks that this oscillation of feeling characterizes Western medieval life in general, an assertion which seems to me in need of qualification. There were, in fact, milieus in which a more moderate temper was believed to be appropriate. The Brethren of the Common Life was one notable example in Northern Europe, and the demeanor of the speakers in Boccaccio's *Decameron* suggests that ancient Roman notions of urbanity and moderation were held in repute in some sophisticated circles of fourteenth-century Italy.

Whatever the truth of Huizinga's general claim, the temperament which permitted and sought out oscillations in mood appears to have been common in Western Europe in the late medieval and early modern period. "It is well known," writes Petit-Dutaillis, "how violent manners were in the fifteenth century, with what brutality passions were assuaged, despite the fear of hell, despite the restraints of class distinctions and the chivalrous sentiment of honor, *despite the bonhomie and gaiety of social relations.*"[3]

Norbert Elias comments:

Not that people were always going around with fierce looks, drawn brows, and martial countenances as the clearly visible symbols of their warlike prowess. On the contrary, a moment ago they were joking, now they

mock each other, one word leads to another, and suddenly from the midst of laughter they find themselves
in the fiercest feud. Much of what appears contradictory to us—the intensity of their piety, the violence of
their fear of hell, their guilt feelings, their penitence,
the immense outbursts of joy and gaiety, the sudden
flaring and uncontrolable force of their hatred and belligerence—all these, like the rapid changes of mood,
are in reality symptoms of the same social and personality structure. The instincts, the emotions were
vented more freely, more directly, more openly than
later. It is only to us, in whom everything is more subdued, moderate, and calculated, and in whom social
taboos are built much more deeply into the fabric of
instinctual life as self-restraints, that this unveiled
intensity of piety, belligerence, or cruelty appears as
contradictory.[4]

From the point of view of more moderate temperaments,
it takes little to set off extreme moods and feelings in a person of the sort described by Huizinga, Petit-Dutaillis, and
Elias. From the point of view of a man or woman whose
temperament seeks states of extreme feeling, however, the
things that provoke such feelings are not minor. The events
and circumstances which call up intense emotions do so
rightly; they are subjectively profound. Why should our feelings not embody our cares and concerns, and do this in ample fashion? If deeply offended, why should we not be intensely angry? If we gain something dearly wanted, why
should we not be gleeful? If things mean a great deal to us,
why should we not have strong feelings about them?
Because, the Puritans felt, the expression of extreme emotions would be discourteous to those around us. The moral
constancy demanded by the Puritan tradition had a strong
social purpose. The Puritan attempt "to subject man to the
supremacy of a purposeful will" and enable him "to maintain and act upon his constant motives"[5] was not primarily

for the benefit of the individual, but for the benefit of others. The steady delight which a husband must take in his wife was not for his benefit so much as for hers.

The reliability of our feelings may, in fact, benefit us—by making us happier with our spouse, by giving us a steady psychic center, or, as with the Cambridge Platonists, by bringing us closer to God. But the direct and originating need for constancy comes from the demand of others. A clear illustration of this truth is the late-seventeenth- and early-eighteenth-century campaign of Steele and his contemporaries to establish good humor as the temperament and mood appropriate to social life and marriage.

In the name of constancy, Steele attacks an ethic which authorizes extreme feelings such as bitter hatred, deep sorrow, great joy, and high rage and which permits rapid and sharp swings from one extreme to another, or quick movements from more moderate states of feelings to one of the extremes. The rapid swing from black sorrow to lively joy, from tenderness to rage, from calm to a cold but burning hatred—these are the targets of his scorn.

While Steele criticizes such extremities of feeling in a general fashion, he seeks above all to change behavior in two specific domains of human relations: marriage and informal relations. He calls the second domain "that part of Life we ordinarily understand by the Word Conversation"; he also calls it "Society" and "Company."[6] It consists of the meetings at parties, coffeehouses, dinners, and the eighteenth-century equivalent of country weekends. I shall call it *social life*, those times one spends with friends, acquaintances, and neighbors, when a main object of participation is to have a good time.

Not an oscillating temper, but a good-humored temper, is appropriate in the presence of spouses and friends. In general, the person with such a temper maintains durable good spirits in the pursuit of his own ends, in his response to the acts of others, and to the circumstances of his life. He is ready and inclined to have life please him. He avoids, as much as possible, ill humor, anger, dark sorrow, intense irri-

tation, gloom—any intensely felt mood or emotion of displeasure. "Whatever we do," writes Steele, "we should keep
up the Chearfulness of our Spirits, and never let them sink
below an Inclination at least to be well pleased."[7]

Steele also advocates the exclusion of intensities of high
joy and delight. Intense joy makes one liable to melancholy.
Addison writes that he

> always preferred Chearfulness to Mirth. . . . Mirth is
> short and transient, Chearfulness fixt and permanent.
> Those are often raised into the greatest Transports of
> Mirth, who are subject to the greatest Depressions of
> Melancholy. On the contrary, Chearfulness, tho' it
> does not give the Mind such an exquisite Gladness,
> prevents us from falling into any Depths of Sorrow. . . .
> [It] keeps up a kind of Day-light in the Mind, and fills it
> with a steady and perpetual Serenity.[8]

Good humor is seen as a moderate temperament which
gives a constant emotional tone to our lives.

Oscillations of feeling are permitted, but they must be
gentle and not carry us to extremes. Anger must be calmed.
This advice is directed particularly at men, who have a natural masculine inclination to rage and "sullen and morose"
moods.[9] Sorrow, too, if it is not too extreme, is no violation
of the good-humored temper. Steele, rewriting a letter from
a recent widower, has the bereaved gentleman say:

> [M]y Sorrow is still fresh; and . . . often, in the midst of
> Company, upon any Circumstance that revives her
> Memory, . . . I am all over Softness, and obliged to re-
> tire, and give way to a few Sighs and Tears, before I can
> be easy. . . . My Concern [troubled state of mind] is not
> indeed so outragious [immoderate] as at the first Trans-
> port; for I think it has subsided rather into a soberer
> State of Mind, than any actual Perturbation of Spirit.
> There might be Rules formed for Men's Behaviour on
> this great Incident, to bring them from that Misfortune
> into the Condition I am at present, which is, I think,

that my Sorrow has converted all Roughness of Temper into Meekness, Good-nature, and Complacency [disposition or wish to please].[10]

This gentle sorrow should be no stranger, thinks Steele, to the audience at the theater: he laments that people make fun of those who weep:

It is indeed prodigious to observe how little Notice is taken of the most exalted Parts of the best Tragedies in *Shakespear;* nay it is not only visible that Sensuality has devoured all Greatness of Soul, but the under Passion (as I may so call it) of a noble Spirit, Pity, seems to be a Stranger to the Generality of an Audience. . . . [With respect to] the Female Part of the Audience . . . what is of all the most to be lamented, is, the Loss of a Party whom it would be worth preserving in their right Senses upon all Occasions, . . . whom we may indifferently call the Innocent or the Unaffected. You may sometimes see one of these sensibly touched with a well wrought Incident; but then she is so impertinently observed by the Men, and frowned at by some insensible Superior of her own Sex, that she is ashamed, and loses the Enjoyment of the most laudable Concern, Pity. Thus the whole Audience is afraid of letting fall a Tear, and shun as a Weakness the best and worthiest Part of our Sense.[11]

Such sweet moderation in feeling, Steele recognizes, may not always be possible. The widower's initial agitation over the loss of his wife appeared excessive, an immoderate disturbance of sobriety and good temper. Steele does not condemn the man; indeed, he often likes to think of scenes where even the good-tempered must give way to extreme emotion. The widower remains an exemplary man of good humor, however, because he seeks to keep his strong feelings from his companions and welcomes his return to a more gentle mood.

Such is the general character of Steele's ethic of good humor. But more is demanded in social life than moderation in feeling and a generally cheerful temper; we must also do what we can to nourish and maintain the good and lively spirits of the company of which we are part. Nothing must weaken a steady good cheer. Therefore, our low or angry moods must be kept to ourselves. The restraint to be exercised upon our words and demeanor extends beyond the expression of feelings. We must not even talk about our aches and pains, no matter how soberly, for this contributes nothing to good cheer.[12] Indeed, when in company we ought to restrain ourselves from talking about any trial or difficulty of our own which would pain others. "That part of Life," writes Steele, "which we ordinarily understand by the Word Conversation, is an Indulgence to the Sociable Part of our Make, and should incline us to bring our proportion of good Will or good Humour among the Friends we meet with, and not trouble them with Relations which must of necessity oblige them to a real or feign'd Affliction."[13]

For the same reason, there is no place for open anger in social life. If it cannot be restrained, one had best leave the fellowship of company until the anger subsides. One must possess, or at the very least appear to possess, a steady feeling which is as important as any overt act of politeness or consideration. The feeling must be natural, spontaneous, and constant. Like the Puritan theory of marriage, Steele's ethic of good humor requires the integration of conscience and impulse.

But the ethic was not primarily for the benefit of the individual, and to protect good humor, a world of private feelings had to be created. Intense or untoward emotions were withdrawn and were nowhere expressed in the words and gestures of social life. All this restraint was for the benefit of others, and not for the person suffering intense sorrow or anger. Good humor, in an obvious way, benefits others by putting them in a like state of mind. It is naturally infectious: "a chearful Mind is not only disposed to be affable and obliging, but raises the same good Humour in those who come within its Influence," says Addison. Steele suggests that the

cheerful man "communicates" his good temper "wherever
he appears." . . . The Sad, the Merry, the Severe, the Melancholy," all "shew a new Chearfulness when he comes
amongst them."[14]

In social life, as Steele sees it, others are not interested in
hearing complaints about aches and pains, or in sharing sorrow and grief. Hot tears or tales of woe are experienced as in-
trusions into the world of others. This is true whether or not
people are much perturbed by them. Of course, one person
might care for another more than social life requires, as
might happen among old friends. But inasmuch as someone
is simply a participant in social life, Steele expects others to
be only casually concerned with his well-being. Thus, at the
root of the demand for good humor in social life is a peculiar
conjunction of attitudes: we must attempt to please and to
take pleasure in others, yet at the same time to lack an interest in their troubles and strong feelings.

In marriage, too, one is required to sustain the cheer and
moderate spirits which characterize good humor.[15] But one
is not required to restrain the expression of sorrow and irritation with the same stringency as within social life. Marriage is a place where sorrows, joys, fears, and hopes should
be shared, a place where one's suffering, even one's intense
grief, may be assuaged through communication and comfort. Portia, the wife of Brutus, is thus an exemplary spouse,
as Steele tells us in *The Christian Hero*, his first publication
devoted to moral reform. Denied the confidences of her
husband, "she gave her self a deep Stab in the Thigh, and
thought if she could bear that Torture" and conceal her pain,
she could keep her husband's secrets. She then confronts her
husband: "I, *Brutus*, being the Daughter of *Cato*, was given
to you in Marriage, not like a Concubine, to partake only of
the common Civilities of Bed and Board, but to bear a Part
in all your good and all your evil Fortunes. . . . But from
Me, what Evidence of my Love, what Satisfaction can you
receive, if I may not share with you in your most hidden
Griefs, nor be admitted to any of your Counsels, that require
Secrecy and Trust."[16]

In a rather different tone, Steele calls for the same sharing of feelings in marriage when he describes the wedded bliss of Florio and Amanda:

> *Amanda* . . . lives in the continual Enjoyment of new Instances of her Husband's Friendship, and sees it as the end of all his Ambition to make her Life one Series of Pleasure and Satisfaction; and *Amanda*'s Relish of the Goods of Life, is all that makes 'em pleasing to *Florio:* They behave themselves to each other when present with a certain apparent Benevolence, which transports above Rapture; and they think of each other in Absence with a Confidence unknown to the highest Friendship: Their Satisfactions are doubled, their Sorrows lessened by Participation.[17]

If our sorrows are to be lessened in this way, we must be able to open ourselves to our spouses and allow them into our hearts, the residence of our sorrows. We must express our griefs, our petty problems and irritations, the small things that make life difficult and painful. Steele greatly admires Cicero because he shares all these things with his wife, Terentia. "Every one," writes Steele, "admires the Orator and the Consul; but for my Part, I esteem the Husband and the Father. His private Character, with all the little Weaknesses of Humanity, is as amiable, as the figure he makes in publick is awful and majestick. . . . [I]t would be barbarous to form to our selves any Idea of Mean-spiritedness from these natural Openings of his Heart, and disburthening of his Thoughts to a Wife."[18]

While marriage, for Steele, permits a degree of emotional freedom not permitted by social life, it would be unwise to contrast these two realms too sharply. They are not like two entirely different games, say baseball and football, each with its own set of rules which cannot be applied to the other game. Marriage and social life are more like two different versions of the same game, or like closely related games; many of the rules overlap. Steele's social life would be an excellent place to learn the cheerful tone which marriage ordinarily requires.

Richard Sennett writes that "the citizens of the 18th Century capitals attempted to define both what public life was and what it was not. The line drawn between public and private was essentially one on which the claims of civility— epitomized by cosmopolitan, public behavior—were balanced against the claims of nature—epitomized by the family. . . . The public realm was a corrective to the private realm" as the private was to the public; "natural man was an animal; the public therefore corrected a deficiency of nature which a life conducted according to the codes of family love alone would produce: this deficiency was incivility. . . . [N]ature's vice was its rudeness."[19]

The writings of Steele do not bear out these judgments. The expression of strong feelings is permitted in marriage, but not in social life. Steele thinks that marriage, unlike social life, is the realm of love, but this hardly makes the family the realm of nature and public life the domain of civility. The man who is ill-tempered on social occasions is a typical object of Steele's humor, but at most he is pictured as a disagreeable type. The ill-tempered man at home receives more severe censure, for he deeply wounds the one who loves him most. Incivility is, for Steele, a more grievous and more poignant offense at home than it is abroad.

In happy marriages, negative feelings toward one's spouse are much less powerful than the feelings of love and devotion, but they do ordinarily exist. The affection and good will which happily married couples feel toward each other is allowed free play by the ethic of good humor, but the antagonism and hostile judgments normally generated by any deep and permanent attachment must be largely repressed. Gentle displeasure or irritation is the maximum acceptable rebuke in a good marriage. "Sweetness of Temper, and Simplicity of Manners," writes Steele, "are the only lasting Charms of Woman." There is

an outragious Species of the Fair Sex which is distinguish'd by the Term Scolds. The Generality of Women are by Nature loquacious: Therefore meer Volubility of Speech is not to be imputed to them, but should be considered with Pleasure when it is used to express such Passions as tend to sweeten or adorn Conversation: But when, through Rage, Females are vehement in their Eloquence, nothing in the World has so ill an Effect upon the Features; for by the Force of it, I have seen the most Amiable become the most Deformed; and she that appeared one of the Graces, immediately turned into one of the Furies.[20]

Husbands as well as wives are condemned for their rages. Steele tells us:

It is a very common Expression, That such a one is very good-natur'd, but very passionate. The Expression indeed is very good-natur'd, to allow passionate People so much Quarter: But I think a passionate Man deserves the least Indulgence imaginable. . . . I have known one of these good-natur'd passionate Men say in a mix'd Company, even to his own Wife or Child, such Things as the most inveterate Enemy of his Family would not have spoke, even in Imagination. . . . To contain the Spirit of Anger, is the worthiest Discipline we can put our selves to. . . . It ought to be the Study of every Man, for his own Quiet and Peace. When he stands combustible and ready to flame upon every thing that touches him, Life is as uneasie to himself as it is to all about him.[21]

Not only uneasiness in oneself and others, but much worse can come from a masculine willingness to fly into a rage. Steele tells the story of Mr. Eustace and his spouse, "a Lady of Youth, Beauty, and Modesty." Mr. Eustace, however, was "in his secret Temper impatient of Rebuke," and his wife was apt to fall into "little Sallies of Passion, yet as suddenly recalled by her own Reflection on her Fault, and the Consideration of her Husband's Temper." This, along with his own restraint on his temper, for a time kept the worst from happening. But once, when in dispute with her, he remained angry even after she had checked her own passion. When they went to bed he feigned sleep, and when she was no longer awake, "he now saw his Opportunity, and with a Dagger he had brought to Bed with him, stabbed his Wife in the Side. She awaked in the highest Terror; but immediately imagined it was a Blow designed for her Husband by Ruffians, began to grasp him, and strive to awake and rouze him to defend himself." Still pretending to sleep, he struck her again. "She now drew open the Curtains, and by the Help of Moon-light saw his Hand lifted up to stab her" one more time. In her horror she could not resist, and his knife plunged into her, this time fatally. "As soon as he believed he had dispatched her, he attempted to escape out of the Window: But she, still alive, called to him not to hurt himself; for she might live." Brought to an even higher rage by her goodness, and his own villany, he stabbed her yet again before he fled. His wife had only enough strength to go to her sister's apartment and tell the story before she died. "Some Weeks after, an Officer of Justice, in attempting to seize the Criminal, fired upon him, as did the Criminal upon the Officer. Both their Balls took Place, and both immediately expired."[22]

This melodramatic story reveals much concerning Steele's beliefs about the relations between man and wife. The gruesome events result from the hot nature of Mr. Eustace, who is apt to fall into a rage upon being rebuked; the passionate sallies of his wife, who cannot resist giving way at times to her own anger; and the deep love of Mrs. Eustace for her husband, which makes her sympathetic to his plight and makes her think of him even as she lies mortally wounded by his hand.

This last quality of Mrs. Eustace's character bears examination, for in the absence of any expression of anger against her husband even after he has stabbed her, she is an exaggerated exemplar of the appropriate feminine response to a husband's anger. At the same time, since she did allow herself to be openly and passionately angry at him in the dispute which led to her death, we can feel that she brought her death upon herself by failing to restrain her own anger. The principle which she at first violates and then heeds is this: if a spouse is angry, do not respond with anger of your own; this will only provoke him further.

In principle, this maxim applies as much to husbands as it does to wives,[23] but in fact the burden of restraint falls more upon women than upon men. Steele thinks that timidity and fear are attractive and excellent features of the feminine sex, qualities worth preserving even if they make women weak. "If we were to form an Image of Dignity in a Man," he writes, "we should give him Wisdom and Valour, as being essential to the Character of Manhood. In like manner, if you describe a right Woman in a laudable Sense, she should have a gentle Softness, tender Fear, and all those parts of Life, which distinguish her from the other Sex, with some Subordination to it, but such an Inferiority that makes her still more lovely."[24] In another place Steele tells us that ladies who rage have a "false Notion . . . of what we call a Modest Woman. They have too narrow a Conception of this lovely Character, and believe they have not at all forfeited their Pretentions to it, provided they have no Imputations on their Chastity." But "Modesty never rages, never murmurs, never pouts: When it is ill-treated, it pines, it beseeches, it languishes."[25] Although anger against one's mate is reprehensible in both husband and wife, its presence in a woman is not only an ethical fault, but a disfigurement of her very sexual being. She is not only unattractive, but unfeminine.

In responding angrily to her husband's ill temper, a woman violates her womanhood as well as the ethic of good humor. Her only legitimate resources are her weakness, her fear, and her charm.[26] Moreover, a woman's weakness is now made a central element of her appeal to a man. The woman who cannot moderate the temper of her ill-humored husband by her frailty is an object of pity, even of tragedy.[27]

For Steele, both the timidity of woman and her capacity to suffer for others make her feminine and thus eligible for a husband's love. Although we all have compassionate tendencies within us, women "are by Nature form'd to Pity, Love and Fear," while men are formed "with an Impulse to Ambition, Danger and Adventure."[28] Mrs. Eustace's story illustrates, in exaggerated fashion, the difficulties a woman may have in holding her own against her husband if she believes that timidity and compassion are special feminine excellencies. As long as the husband is good-humored, no difficulty arises, but when he is in a bad mood or morose, it is easy for a wife to end up doing little but weep, as Steele has one unhappy wife do.[29]

The allocation of emotions sustains both the stability and the hierarchy of marriage. But the appropriate male and female feelings cannot last long without a hierarchy of economic power to support them. A woman, says Steele, must be weaker both emotionally and financially. Thus he roundly condemns agreements made at the time of marriage which give a wife some economic independence from her husband. It was common practice for the husband to oblige himself by periodically providing his wife with a certain sum of money to use as she saw fit ("pin money"), to assign a certain portion of his estate to her use in the event of her widowhood (a "jointure"), or to settle a certain portion of his estate (or his wife's) upon the children of their marriage when, for example, they come of age. Steele condemns all these arrangements.[30] Such marriage contracts, he objects, make "even Beauty and Virtue the Purchase of Money."[31] This objection soon gives way to another: marriage settlements reduce the dependency of wife upon husband, a dependency which is the basis of marital love. As Steele has Sir Harry Gubbin say, pin money is the "Foundation of Wives Rebellion, and Husband's Cuckoldom."[32] A woman should trust her husband's feelings of love and concern for her and for their children; those feelings should be seen as the source of his actions toward them. But feelings are not looked to when pin money and jointures are sought. "Thus is Tenderness thrown out of the Question; and the great Care is, What the young Couple shall do when they come to hate each other?"[33]

To be happy in marriage, a wife must look to nothing but the goodness and feeling of her husband. Yet a man need not rely solely on the feelings of his wife and children. He should wield the power of the purse to bring them to act as they should. Thus, Steele objects to marriage arrangements which make wives financially independent, for such arrangements deprive the man of power to encourage the behavior he wants. "The Coldness of Wives to their Husbands, as well as Disrespect from Children to Parents," he writes, "arise from this one Source."[34] There is an obvious imbalance in the powers Steele would give to women and to men.

If a man who has the financial upper hand can be trusted to deal properly with his wife and children just because of his natural sentiments, why should a wife not be trusted to do the same with her husband and children, assuming she had a similar independence? What harm could come to marriage if spouses were equally powerful and equally independent? Steele cannot accept such equality; he cannot see an intense emotional disagreement in married love settled in any way but by the subordination of wife to husband. He "cannot, with all the Help of Science and Astrology, find any other Remedy" for "Conjugal Enmity" but the one he finds in Milton's *Paradise Lost:* husband and wife must realize that they are "both weak, but one weaker than the other."[35] He knows of no emotional script for equals that holds out hope of reconciliation.

This attitude is reminiscent of Locke, who wrote that in cases of marital dispute "the Rule" must be placed somewhere, and it naturally falls to the man. Just as in Locke's case, Steele's view requires explanation, since Steele was quite familiar with modes for the resolution of disagreements between equals. Friendship, after all, is often a relation between equals (Aristotle said it had to be that), but friends find ways to settle disputes. In truth, hierarchy is not a solution to the difficulties of marriage for Steele. He wants it for its own sake.

But Steele's ethic of good humor is not designed simply to sustain the authority of the husband. It is also meant to make emotional relations more stable and calm—both among equals, as in social life, and among superior and inferior, as in marriage. His attitude comes from a fear of and a desire for human relations based on spontaneous feeling. What would social life or marriage be if it did not have a spontaneous yet ethical quality? It would lack the charm and relaxed spirit he so much loves. But feeling is also the source of difficulty in social life and marriage, and Steele fears the expression of intense emotions which might provoke an exchange and an escalation of feeling beyond the control of all concerned.

So our question becomes not why Steele is so intent on restraining the expression of extreme feelings in social life and marriage, but why he is intent on restraining extreme negative feelings. One reason is clear. He believes repression is necessary for stable and constructive social relations. As a young military officer in London, Steele was well acquainted with a milieu in which the oscillating temperament was dominant. His career as a journalist with moral reform as his aim began when he rejected the ethic of this world, whose customs, such as dueling, were built around the grand expression of extremes of emotion. Steele cannot imagine a form of life in which the mutual expression of negative feelings will serve rather than hinder the permanence and goodness of human relations. Anger meeting anger can only lead to worse, not better. Given his conception of the price to be paid for the free expression of negative emotions, it is not surprising that Steele advocates systematic restraint. But there is a price for those who live by his ethic, too: a drastic decrease in the opportunities for emotional discharge.

Men and women with oscillating tempers have strong and rapidly changing feelings. They are also willing in many cases to discharge their full feelings before others, and to do so without any assurance or even expectation that those about them will respond sympathetically. Although the open display of intense suffering was permitted in fifteenth-century Burgundy, the suffering itself was often treated with a thorough indifference, even taunted. "On the one hand," Huizinga writes, "the sick, the poor, the insane, are objects of that deeply moved pity, born of a feeling of fraternity akin to that which is so strikingly expressed in modern Russian literature; on the other hand, they are treated with incredible hardness or cruelly mocked." Thus Pierre de Fenin (d. 1506), who chronicled the murderous rivalry between the houses of Burgundy and Orléans, concludes his description of the death of a gang of brigands by writing, "and the people laughed a good deal, because they were all poor men."[36]

It must have been a peculiarly painful thing to have a display of one's personal feelings ignored. Much open discharge of emotion was just that: discharge, vented without the aim of moving others. Like the person who tells you his troubles no matter what, the fifteenth-century Burgundian who cried in pain or yelled in joy over some personal concern, may not have cared whether anybody was listening. Emotional expression, as opposed to pure discharge, is designed to move others to desired responses. The Burgundians had many ways to express their feelings over mutual concerns: through ringing bells, wearing costumes, or marching in processions. Although an interest in expressing feelings about more personal matters was by no means absent, as the poets of the time make clear, the need to discharge them seems to have overshadowed an interest in their expression.

The world of the oscillating temperament may have waned with the waning of the middle ages, but it did not disappear. Opposing it, Steele demands that we pay attention, in a reliable way, to the feelings of others in social life and marriage. He is sensitive to the pain we suffer if others do not respond sympathetically to the feelings we show.

Steele was not the first to oppose the emotionally unstable world of the oscillating temperament. His ethic of good humor is part of a larger movement of manners in Western Europe from the sixteenth to the eighteenth centuries, which has been described by Norbert Elias. In this movement, there is an increase in the degree and scope of self-restraint required in a number of matters, including one's

behavior at table, one's attitude toward the natural functions, blowing one's nose, and spitting. A demand for what
we might loosely call an increased social orientation is at
work in this movement of manners, in the form of two related principles. First, an interest in the well-being of others
must be shown by restricting the extent to which one's own
body, smells, dirt, and feelings are made present to them.
Second, the interest in one's own body and feelings must be
reduced, and one's concern for what is of general value to
the company of which one is a part must be increased.

These principles of restraint were advocated by Erasmus,
who played an important part in the advance of European
manners through his primer of Latin style for youths, the
Colloquies. In his dialogue on inns, published in the *Colloquies* of 1523, Erasmus provides this description of a typical
German public house: When you arrive, no one greets you,
"lest they seem to be looking for a guest."[37] After much
shouting on your part, someone finally comes out, and you
are brought into a crowded place, called the "stove room,"
where "there are often eighty or ninety met together" for a
meal. This is also the room where people change and wash
after their travels, but the water you wash with may be
dirtier than you are.

At such an inn, it is difficult to rid oneself of one's dirt
and no easier to avoid the dirt of others. In the common
room, full of people, "one combs his hair, another wipes the
sweat off, another cleans his rawhide boots or his leggings,
another belches garlic." The room is so hot that a great stink
arises; the stink gains power from the belches, farts, and foul
breaths of all the occupants of the crowded room.

The Germans do not complain. As Erasmus has one
speaker say, "This is their custom."[38] Perhaps they do not
notice; perhaps the dirt and smells of others do not intrude
on their experience. But they do intrude on the experience of
Erasmus, and he finds the Germans' unwillingness to restrain themselves distasteful. It is gross to belch garlic,
break wind, or have a stinking breath in company. He objects to being forced to experience another's smell or dirt; he

feels it as an invasion or intrusion. He thus thinks that we ought to restrain our bodily presence in company for the sake of others; this is part of good manners. As Elias suggests, Erasmus' attitude is rooted in a sense of his own separateness from his fellow men and women, a separateness which he thinks they ought to respect.

Die Hofzucht, a thirteenth-century poem of courtly good manners attributed to Tannhäuser, says that "a man who clears his throat when he eats and one who blows his nose in the tablecloth are both ill-bred." But one should not suppose that handkerchiefs were to be used instead, for, as Elias says, they did not yet exist.[39] In the Western world, they first appeared in Renaissance Italy among the fancy young men of the nobility. Before that, one simply blew one's nose on one's sleeve or in one's hands. When the handkerchief was introduced, not everybody knew how to use it or used it in the way which advanced theorists of manners thought appropriate. Della Casa, a major sixteenth-century authority on manners, instructed both children and adults that when they blew their nose in their handkerchief, they should not then look at what was in the handkerchief as if it were pearls and rubies.

As for urination and defecation, the following passages occur in the Wernigerode Court Regulations of 1570: "One should not, like rustics who have not been to court or lived among refined and honorable people, relieve oneself without shame or reserve in front of ladies, or before the doors or windows of court chambers or other rooms. Rather, everyone ought at all times and in all places to show himself reasonable, courteous, and respectful in word and gesture." A passage from the Braunschweig Court Regulations of 1589 insists: "Let no one, whoever he may be, before, at, or after meals, early or late, foul the staircases, corridors, or closets with urine or other filth, but go to suitable, prescribed places for such relief."[40] What at one time were regulations for courtly behavior, addressed to adults and calling for conduct which it was explicitly acknowledged was not to be found in rustic milieus, are today universal notions of conduct. No

Western book of manners would be likely to mention them—not even a book of manners for children—for parents "naturally" bring their children up to heed these rules before the age at which they read. Erasmus tells boys:

> There are those who teach that the boy should retain wind by compressing the belly. Yet it is not pleasing, while striving to appear urbane, to contract an illness. If it is possible to withdraw, it should be done alone. But if not, in accordance with the ancient proverb, let a cough hide the sound.[41]

Today one would not consider a concern not to break wind in company an aspect of urbanity; it would be plain good manners. Erasmus is more relaxed about the matter than Saint Jean-Baptiste de La Salle, author of *Les Règles de la bienséance et de la civilité chrétienne*, who tells his adult readers: *"It is very impolite to emit wind from your body when in company, either from above or below, even if it is done without noise;* and it is shameful and indecent to do it in a way that can be heard by others."[42] Neither the smell nor the noise is at all acceptable in company, under any circumstances.

Consider, finally, the matter of serving oneself from a common dish. Elias describes the manner of eating customary in Erasmus' time:

> Everyone, from the king and queen to the peasant and his wife, eats with the hands. In the upper class there are more refined forms of this. One ought to wash one's hands before a meal, says Erasmus. But there is as yet no soap for this purpose. . . . In good society one does not put both hands into the dish. It is most refined to use only three fingers of the hand. . . . Forks scarcely exist, or at most for taking meat from the dish.[43]

The distinction between utensils for eating and those for serving is not yet very definite: Erasmus says that "if you are offered something liquid, taste it and return the spoon, but first wipe it on your serviette."[44]

Antoine de Courtin, in his *Nouveau traité de civilité*, begins with instructions similar to those of Erasmus: "[Y]ou should always wipe your spoon when, after using it, you want to take something from another dish, there being people so delicate that they would not wish to eat soup into which you had dipped it after putting it into your mouth." But times had changed in the intervening 150 years, for the author adds, "[I]f you are at the table of very refined people, it is not enough to wipe your spoon; you should not use it but ask for another. Also, in many places, spoons are brought in with the dishes, and these serve only for taking soup and sauce."[45] Courtin does not even bother to warn his readers that "to dip the fingers in the sauce is rustic," as Erasmus had to do.[46]

It should not be startling to note that one ordinarily has far greater tolerance for one's own smell and dirt than for the smell and dirt of others. But this extreme sensitivity to the body odors of others and the correlative self-restraint exercised today are far greater than that required by the manuals of medieval Western Europe. People found the excreta and odors of others less distasteful and seem to have noticed them less. Erasmus' observations were not shared by his fellow lodgers at the German inn, but the sensitivity which he exemplifies was on the increase as manners developed in late medieval and early modern Europe.

The ethic of good humor which Steele makes the basis of social life is, then, a natural extension of the general principles at work in late medieval and early modern Western European manners. Steele moves from notions of how to use a spoon and blow one's nose to ideas about how much one should feel, how much feelings should be expressed, and whether one should tell of one's troubles in society.[47] He thinks of intense feelings the way Erasmus thinks of dirt and smells: in social life, others are intruded upon if these feelings are made vividly present to them. In the social realm, the expression of strong feelings would be as intrusive to Steele as the fart was to La Salle: one does not want to have to know anybody in such an intimate way. There is in Steele's conception of social life, as there is in the conception of manners found in Erasmus, a notion that respect for others is shown through a self-restrained demeanor; I show my respect for you by limiting the extent to which you must experience me. Steele condemns self-absorption on social occasions the way the authors of the conduct books derided looking at the contents of one's handkerchief.

But why shouldn't one look? It does not violate the principle of self-restraint in company, for in looking at one's own snot one need not force it upon another. It can be arranged so that it is seen only by oneself. In looking, however, one violates the restriction upon self-involvement. One must have a concern for, and take interest in, those matters of general value to the company of which one is a part. One's snot, nail-parings, and earwax may interest oneself, but none of them will be of value to others. One must not fall into even a momentary reverie centered around something of value only to oneself.

For the same reason, Steele forbids self-absorption when in society; one must not speak about one's aches and pains or lose oneself in deep sorrow. The bereaved widower must retire from company, for he can no longer attend to the needs and good humor of others.

The new demand for restraint of bodily and emotional presence establishes the realm of private feelings which ordinarily only the individual or those truly intimate with him can know.

The idea of such a personal and interior realm (one component of the modern concept of the individual) is not, as is commonly thought, a product of Romanticism. It derives from the Puritan and early-eighteenth-century concern for stability in human relations. Today, a socially recognized realm of privacy is characteristically deemed a good thing for the individual who possesses that privacy. The roots of this idea lie in the Romantic movement, for modernity has reversed the argument for a socially recognized realm of privacy as it was developed by Steele.

Elias titles the book in which he describes this movement of manners *The Civilizing Process*. This expression was used by Freud to describe the power of art, religion, manners, and other forms of civilized life to create larger and larger social units in which people are joined together by a sense of unity and a common will to be humane to one another. This power, Freud thinks, is active in all of human history. It is ingenious of Elias to borrow this term to name the process he sees at work in the medieval and early modern growth of manners, but he has a very different understanding of what the goals of the civilizing process are.

For Freud, the process of civilization was ultimately at the service of Eros, which seeks to unite the hearts and minds of people. Eros aims at a spiritual and mental unity, not simply at the establishment of collectivities united by civility and individual restraint. All that Elias sees at work in the history of manners in early modern Europe is an increased self-restraint which permits larger and larger social and political collectivities. I believe Freud's is the more accurate perception.

It is true that the ethic of good humor and the manners described by Elias have as their object emotional and even bodily separation between people. The feelings of others should not intrude into one's experience, just as their smells should not. If this goal is considered on its own, it would appear that the civilizing process has as its only end a world of civility and stability built on restraint and the emotional separation of individuals. The matter looks otherwise, though, if the manners and ethic of good humor are seen as answering a demand for constancy in feeling and attitude which has as its purpose the union of people in mind and spirit. Husbands and wives who comply with Steele's demand for the restraint of negative feelings (not only in behavior but internally) are united by a devotion to common repression. They share a common conscience. Inasmuch as this conscience is to function in a constant and thorough manner—for the power of conscience in table manners and social behavior is meant to be so integrated with the rest of an individual's character that nothing can break its hold—they share a constant sense of right and wrong which is unremitting in its force. In the details of daily life, conscience is now thoroughly in control; it unites people, and so serves the purpose of Eros. But the instinctive renunciation required for social stability and mental union is hardly trivial. English culture did not simply leave people to their own devices in their attempts to compensate themselves for the emotional deprivation they suffered in order to be "good." At least men, to put it more accurately, were not left to fend for themselves in this new and demanding moral regime. The hierarchy between male and female which Steele elaborated appears to be a way in which eighteenth-century English culture freed males from the full costs of moral constancy—a matter which will be more fully explored in the next chapters.

4

Puritan Marriage and the History of Friendship

To call someone Puritan today is to suggest that he is against pleasure, especially sexual pleasure; that he has a repressive attitude toward the body and its functions; that he uses self-discipline to master unacceptable impulses; and that he not only represses his own instinctive life, but that of others as well. In short, he is a bluenose.

In spite of much evidence to the contrary—some of which has been revealed in the foregoing chapters—the conviction persists that the modern idea of a Puritan accurately describes the character of the seventeenth-century Puritans who settled New England. This belief is supported by the authority of Max Weber and his thesis that sixteenth- and seventeenth-century Puritanism was ascetic through and through; that Puritans rejected the human desire for the world and its pleasures in favor of a disciplined obedience to God's will on this earth and the hope of eternal bliss in the life to come.

The aim of Puritan asceticism, says Weber, was an ethically self-disciplined life; its most urgent task was "the destruction of spontaneous, impulsive enjoyment." It fought with all its force against the natural man. In place of spontaneity it called for a life of "cool reserve" and "quiet self-control."[1] This world-rejecting outlook, Weber believes, persisted in American and English life long after Puritanism in its full religious dimension had ceased to be a significant force. He sees it in the economic ethic of Benjamin Franklin, an ethic which required a thoroughly self-disciplined life devoted to the making of "more and more money" while at the same time demanding a "strict avoidance of all spontaneous enjoyment of life."[2] Franklin lacked the Puritans' anxiety about salvation, but he retained their asceticism and their rigorous self-control.

In one respect, at least, Weber is entirely mistaken. Puritanism has at its very heart an ethic which is world-affirming. In their philosophy of marriage—one of the most important domains of life for Puritanism—preachers and theologians call for spontaneous enjoyment, sexual pleasure, and mutual delight. They affirm the intrinsic worth of the delight and comfort which spouses can give to one another. In their view, these pleasures need not be justified by some further spiritual use (although they do think marriage has spiritual purposes); the joys of marriage are goods in themselves, answering the natural human need for companionship and love. Puritanism cannot, therefore, be seen as a thoroughly ascetic religion.

Weber is, on the other hand, correct about the Puritans' demand for thorough self-discipline. In all areas of life— marriage, work, politics, the family, war—Puritan preachers called for systematic self-discipline directed toward the creation of constant and reliable motives. This applied as much to the love of one's spouse as to the restraint to be exercised in one's enjoyment of wealth and worldly goods. The call to moral constancy did have ascetic consequences whenever the pleasures of the world were seen to require an abandonment of self-discipline and moral steadiness.

Mainstream Puritans did not see marital sexuality as a threat to moral constancy; in fact, they saw it as a remarkable and happy harmony of carnal, moral, and spiritual bonds. But eighteenth- and nineteenth-century English Dissenters and Evangelicals often took an opposing view. Puritanism has become synonymous with hostility to pleasure—particularly sexual pleasure—because those who are regarded as its heirs viewed constancy and self-discipline as requiring extreme degrees of sexual renunciation.

One must concede that the Puritans maintained the highest standards and ideals. They demanded of themselves and of others a life which was, in the realm of everyday conduct, ethically strict; in the realm of belief, meticulously scrupulous; in matters of ritual, simple (thus they were suspicious of cross and miter, surplice and relic); and in matters of piety, deeply concerned with the inward state of the soul (thus they were hostile to a church satisfied with the perfunctory performance of outward acts).[3] This piety had its analogue in the Puritans' notion of conjugal love. An outward fulfillment of the duties of marriage was not enough; the proper intentions and feelings toward one's spouse were also required.

A few reflections on the Roman Catholic background of Puritan ideas will put the Puritan concept of marriage into perspective. The Roman Catechism of 1566, "a careful distillation of Counter-Reformation theology,"[4] exhorts men and women, in marrying, to seek at least one of these stated ends—though they may seek other ends as well.

The first appropriate end is the

> very partnership of diverse sexes—sought by natural instinct, and compacted in the hope of mutual help so that one aided by the other may more easily bear the discomforts of life and sustain the weakness of old age. Another is the appetite of procreation, not so much indeed that heirs of property and riches be left, but that worshippers of the true faith and religion be educated. . . . And this is the one cause why God instituted marriage at the beginning. . . . The third is one which after the Fall of the first parent was added to the other causes, . . . [for man's] appetite began to fight with right reason; so indeed he who is conscious of his weakness and does not wish to bear the battle of the flesh may use the remedy of marriage to avoid sins of lust.[5]

In making companionship (specifically, mutual support and comfort) one of the chief purposes of marriage, and in listing companionship first among these purposes, the authors of the catechism went against Augustine and others within the Catholic world who made little of this particular feature of marriage.

Genesis 2.18–23 tells us that God did not find it good for man to be alone and therefore gave Adam a helpmeet: woman, bone of his bone, flesh of his flesh. She pleased him greatly. But why, asks Augustine, did Adam need a *woman* to be his helpmeet? As far as he can see, she would have been of no use to him, or any man, if she had not been capable of bearing children.[6] What of woman as delightful companion, comforter, and supporter to man? What of man as this to woman? Companionship receives scant mention in the theology of Augustine. In his commentary on Genesis 9.7, he repeats what he had said some years before in *De Bono Coniugale:* the goods of marriage are three: *fides, proles, sacramentum. Fides,* fidelity, includes paying the marriage debt as well as refraining from intercourse with others; *proles,* the good of offspring, includes the support and education of children as well as their creation; marriage is a *sacramentum,* a symbol of stability, therefore indissoluble. None of these goods, as Noonan convincingly argues, includes the delight in the companionship and comfort which a man and a woman can give to each other.[7]

Within the medieval and early modern Roman Church, Aristotle's *Nichomachean Ethics* sustained those who sought to give a more honored place to marriage as friendship. In the *Ethics,* Aristotle says that marriage is a kind of friendship, indeed one more natural to human beings than the friendship of those who constitute the polis. We are by nature political animals, but we are even more inclined to form couples than we are to form cities.[8] Friends can be useful to each other, they can delight in one another's company, and they can love one another's virtue. All three grounds are available to the married couple. Spouses can be useful to each other in the running of a household, they can please and delight each other in their sexual relations, and they can love one another's virtue, if they are virtuous.[9] Marital love is special, for it can unite into one all the kinds of friendship we can ever have. Virtuous men can love each other for their virtue; youths typically love each other for sheer pleasure; old men may be friends because it is useful to them. Spouses, however, may love one another for all these reasons at any stage of life.

The idea of marriage as friendship is taken up by Saint Thomas.[10] He relies upon Aristotle's notion that there must be a certain equality in all relationships to defend his belief that a man can have only one wife at a time. If reason deems it improper for a woman to have several husbands at one time, then, Thomas argues, it is wrong for a man to have several wives at one time. Marriage is a friendship, and equality is a condition of friendship. "Were it lawful for a man to have several wives," but not lawful for a wife to have several husbands, "the friendship of a wife for her husband would not be freely bestowed, but servile as it were," for she would not be his true equal; "and this argument," says Thomas, "is confirmed by experience: since where men have several wives, the wives are treated as servants." He also writes, "The greatest friendship" seems to be between spouses, for husband and wife "are made one not only in the act of carnal intercourse, which even among dumb animals causes an agreeable fellowship, but also as partners in the whole intercourse of daily life: so that, to indicate this, man must *leave father and mother* (Gen. 2.24) for his wife's sake."[11]

The same belief that marriage is a friendship and a source of mutual delight and comfort sustains some of the liberalizing tendencies within the late medieval and early modern church concerning sexual delight within marriage. Augustine takes the position that God warrants and permits the pleasure of intercourse among spouses only to the extent that it furthers the end of procreation: "What food is for the health of man, intercourse is for the health of the species, and each is not without carnal delight which cannot be lust, if modified and restrained by temperance, it is brought to a natural use," that is, done for the sake of procreation.[12] Unlike Aristotle, he does not think of sexual delight as a constituent of marital friendship. Aristotle's belief, however, remains alive in spite of Augustine. It is fully presented by Thomas in his commentary on the *Ethics;* moreover, Thomas accepts Aristotle's outlook, although he makes little use of it, in *Summa Contra Gentiles* 3.123.

The Scotsman John Major, professor of theology at the Universities of Paris, Glasgow, and Saint Andrews during the first half of the sixteenth century, is more in accord with Aristotle's view. In his commentary on the sentences of Peter Lombard, he writes: "Whatever men say, it is difficult to prove that a man sins in knowing his own wife for the sake of having pleasure," for husband and wife marry not only to have children, but to provide "consolation" to one another.[13] The defense of this opinion in the seventeenth century provoked fierce opposition from rigorists within the Church, especially the theologians of Louvain, led by the Irishman John Sinnigh, who called the opinion permitting intercourse for pleasure "brutish."[14]

Major did not go so far as to make the life of the married equal or superior in merit to the life of committed celibates. But the doctrine that celibacy is the superior state, defended by writers like Jerome and Chrysostom in the ancient world[15] and upheld by Thomas (close as he was to Aristotle), was to be vigorously challenged in the sixteenth century, most notably by Erasmus. What could be more honorable or holy than matrimony, he asks in his *Encomium Matrimonii,* since its author was not Lycurgus, Moses, or Solon, but God himself?[16]

> For at the begynnyng when he had made man of the slyme of the earthe he thought that his lyfe shoulde be utterly myserable and unpleasaunt, if he joyned not Eve a compagnion unto him. . . . Now syr if the other sacramentes of Christes chyrch be had in great veneration, who seeth nat that moch worshyppe ought to be

gyven to this, which was both ordeyned of god, & fyrst of all other? And the other in erth, this is paradise / the other for remedy / this for solas / the other were put to in helpe of nature . . . which was fallen, only this was gyven to nature at the fyrst creation.[17]

"Bacherlershyp," Erasmus tells a friend who is unwilling to marry, is "a forme of lyvnge bothe barren and unnaturall" (A4r), whereas nothing could be more natural than wedlock, so much so that all peoples, no matter how barbarous, deem it holy.[18] God has deeply imprinted the need and desire for marital love not only upon us but upon other species, for "the sense and feelynge" of marital love "hath not only perced the turtyls / and the doves / but also the most cruell wyld bestes. For the lyons be gentil and meeke to theyr lyonnesses." Whosoever, therefore, "is nat touched with desyr of wedlocke seemeth to be no man, but a stone / an ennemy to nature / a rebelle to god / by his owne foly sekynge hys decay and undoynge" ([B6r], B4v).

Christ said that those who gelded themselves for the kingdom of God were blessed (Matt. 19), but his words appertained only to those times "when it was expedient to be most redy and lose from all worldly bussynesses." Today, Erasmus says, "the most holy kynd of lyfe is wedlocke puerly & chastly kept" (C1v). And in this bond, duty and pleasure need not be enemies: "[I]f the most parte of thynges (yea whyche be also bytter) ar of a good man to be desyred for none other purpose, but bycause they be honeste, matrimony doutles is chefely to be desyred whereof a man may dout whether it hath more honesty than pleasure[.] For what thynge is sweeter, then with her to lyve, with whome ye may be most streyghtly copuled, nat onely in the benevolence of the mynd, but also in the conjunction of the body" ([C6r]). The "plesure of bodyes is the leste parte of the goodes that wedlock hathe," yet it is not to be despised ([C8v]).

"It has . . . bene rightly every where pronounced as a proverbe, that *god nor nature have made no thynge frustrate nor in vayne* / why (I pray you) hath god geven us these members? why these pryckes and provocations? why hath he added the power of begettynge, if bachelarshyp be taken for a prayse?" ([B7v]). The body is meant to be used. "If one wold gyve you a pretious gyfte, as a bowe / a garment / or a swerde, ye shuld seme unworthy [of] the thyng that ye have receyved, if outher ye wolde nat, or ye could nat use it" ([B7v]). He who is not taken with the pleasures of earthly love—so sweetly coupled with fond devotion within marriage—"I wold cal hym no man but a playne stone" ([C8v]). Nothing can be said for the man content with bachelorhood. "[W]hat is more hatefull then the man which (as though he were borne onely to hymself) . . . loveth no persone, is loved of no persone?" ([C8r]).

Erasmus was not alone in his advocacy of the superiority of the married state over virginity; Vives took the same position, and Todd argues that a substantial number of sixteenth-century Catholics and Anglicans did the same.[19] Yet the fate of these ideas of Erasmus was not altogether a happy one. On the Continent, the Council of Trent declared the view that marriage is superior to celibacy "anathema," and in 1547 the Sorbonne put the *Encomium Matrimonii* on the index of prohibited books.[20] In the large catechism of Cardinal Bellarmine, the *Ample Declaration of the Christian Faith* (English translation, 1604), of great influence in the seventeenth-century Church, the student asks "whether it be better to take the Sacrament of Matrimonie or to kepe virginitie?" The Master replies,

> The Apostel S. Paul hath cleared this doubt, having written that he who joyneth himself in Mariage doth wel, but he that doth not joyne himself, but kepeth virginitie doth better. And the reason is, because Mariage is a thing humane, virginitie is Angelical. Mariage is according to nature, Virginitie is above nature. And not only virginitie but widowhood is also better than mariage. Therefore whereas our Saviour said in a para-

ble, that the good sede yelded in one fild thirtie fold
fruite, in an other threeschore, in an other a hundred
fold: the holie Doctors have declared, that the thirtie
fold fruite is of Matrimonie, the threescore fold of widowhood, the hundreth fold of virginitie.[21]

In England, whose humanists had perhaps taught Erasmus something about marriage, the notion of marriage as
the best sort of friendship—as a union of erotic, spiritual,
domestic, and ethical bonds—and the idea that it is the best
sort of life for man and woman, were more successful, no
doubt owing to the Church of England's abolition of monastic orders and of the requirement of celibacy for the secular
priest. From the second half of the sixteenth century, students at Oxford and Cambridge encountered a university
curriculum that included works by Erasmus, Vives, and
Thomas More. Preachers cited them, and the scholarly and
pious included their works in their private collections. And
from the 1620s to the 1660s, a flood of often superbly written texts on marriage came forth, largely from Puritan
pens.[22]

These writers—Thomas Gataker, William Gouge, Richard Baxter, and Daniel Rogers among them—celebrated
marriage. "Let al[l] Papists, Jesuites, Priests or others,"
writes Rogers, "with all their formenters and adherents,
tremble and be ashamed, who have dared so many times to
dishonour marriage, and so many wayes to defile it." "They
know not the benefit of the married estate," writes Gouge,
"who prefer single life before it." He calls upon the "admir-
eres and praisers of a single estate" to "bring forth all their
reasons, and put them in the other scole against marriage.
If these two be duly poised, and rightly weyed, we should
find single life too light to be compared with honest
marriage."[23]

What is so good about married life? Gouge, offering a trin-
ity of reasons already well established within the Catholic
and Anglican world, says it is for procreation, the avoidance

of fornication, and mutual aid: "No such helpe," he writes, "can man have from any other creature as from a wife; or a woman, as from an husband."[24]

Like Erasmus, Puritans argue for the excellence of marriage by pointing out that it was instituted by God before humankind had fallen; it was not simply a remedy for our concupiscence (though it became that once we fell). It was part of the paradisiacal state itself.[25] But why did Adam need a wife? Why did he need to better his condition in this way? What was wrong with Paradise without Eve? The Puritans do not share the outlook of Augustine, who thought that she would have been of no use to Adam had she not been the bearer of his children. For the Puritans, she was also his companion; it was not good that he was alone (Gen. 2.18), and he needed a woman for a companion, as she needed a man. Secker puts it well:

> When all other creatures had their mates, *Adam* wanted his: Though he was the Emperor of the Earth, and the Admiral of the Seas, yet in Paradise without a companion, though he was truly happy, yet he was not fully happy; Though he had enough for his board, yet he had not enough for his bed; Though he had many creatures to serve him, yet he wanted a creature to solace him; when he was compounded in Creation, he must be compleated by conjunction; when he had no sinne to hurt him, then he must have a wife to help him; *It is not good that man should be alone.*[26]

Therefore, God determined to make him a helpmeet. But as Gouge writes, none of the birds or beasts that God had already created would do, so He created woman out of "mans substance and side, and after his image." Her maker then presented Eve to Adam for his consideration. The first man manifested "a good liking to her," so God gave her to him "to bee his wife." Thus "the inviolable law of the neer and firm union of man and wife is enacted."[27]

It is true that before Adam had Eve, he had God, but this was not enough to rid him of loneliness; nor could this loneliness be assuaged by the creatures that already "lived on the earth, or breathed the aire."[28] He needed a woman, and when a woman was created, she needed a man. The cure for Adam's loneliness was to be love: his love for Eve and her love for him. Eve's loneliness would be cured in the same way. Marriage provides this balm. The Puritans say that men must love their wives, and wives their husbands; Baxter writes in firm tones that *"the first Duty of Husbands is to Love their Wives (and Wives their Husbands) with a true intire Conjugal Love."*[29]

The Puritans' appreciation of conjugal love and the pleasures and comforts of a happily married life was accompanied by an acute awareness of how bad a bad marriage could be. Marriage, writes Gataker, "is *a businesse* of the *greatest consequence,* and that whereon the maine comfort or discomfort of a mans life doth depend; that which may make *thine house* to bee as *an heaven* or *an hell* here upon earth."[30]

"[T]hey that enter into the state of marriage," writes Taylor, who is in accord with the Puritans on this matter, "cast a dye of the greatest contingency, and yet of the greatest interest in the world, next to the last throw for Eternity." A happy marriage provides a joy that lasts throughout life; an unhappy one creates lasting sorrow for both spouses. A wife "hath no Sanctuary to retire to from an evil Husband"; she must remain at home, the very source of her unhappiness, to "dwell upon her Sorrow." A husband can run "from many hours of his saddness, yet he must return to it again, and when he sits among his neighbours, he remembers the objection that lies in his bosom, and he sighs deeply."[31]

Puritan authors sometimes refer to the words of Augustine, who on more than one occasion wrote that a bad marriage is like a bad conscience: you cannot get away from it. When love is absent between husband and wife, writes Baxter, it is like "a Bone out of joynt; there is no *ease,* no *order"* between them till they are set right again.[32]

The love required in marriage is more than a general

goodwill or benevolence towards one's spouse, more than the Christian charity one may bear toward many. It is a special sort of love.[33] For one thing, as Erasmus had indicated, it is sensual as well as spiritual. Marriage is instituted to provide mutual support and comfort; sensuous delight in the body of one's spouse is an essential element of the comfort which marriage must provide. To take (and encourage) delight is thus a duty which falls equally on both spouses. The Puritans who uphold this view, far from being hostile to romance, make romance a duty of married life.[34]

Lucy Hutchinson, the wife of a Puritan soldier and herself a Puritan brought up in a Puritan household, begins her description of the physical appearance of her late husband in the following way, in a memoir of him prepared for the benefit of their children:

> He was of middle stature, of a slender and exactly well-proportioned shape in all parts, his complexion fair, his hair of light brown, very thick set in his youth, softer than the finest silk, and curling into loose great rings at the ends; his eyes of a lively grey, well-shaped and full of life and vigour, graced with many becoming motions; his visage thin, his mouth well made, his lips very ruddy and graceful, although the nether chap shut over the upper, yet it was in such a manner as was not unbecoming; his teeth were even and white as the purest ivory, his chin was something long, and the mould of his face; his forehead was not very high; his nose was raised and sharp; but withal he had a most amiable countenance, which carried in it something of magnanimity and majesty mixed with sweetness, that at the same time bespoke love and awe in all that saw him; his skin was smooth and white, his legs and feet excellently well-made; he was quick in his pace and turns, nimble and active and graceful in all his motions; he was apt for any bodily exercise, and any that he did became him; he could dance admirably well, but

neither in youth nor riper years made any practice of
it.[35]

She goes on to describe other admirable qualities, including
those he possessed in music, dress, and wit. A separate and
major section of her memoir is devoted to his moral and
spiritual virtues.

Her description of her husband no doubt owes much to
modes of thought and perception that do not have their origins in Puritan culture. She is familiar with elements of the
culture of the court, which owed much to the aristocratic
manners and arts of the Continent. Her father was a gentleman who had spent time at court; she herself grew up in the
precincts of the Tower of London, where her father was
lieutenant.[36]

She writes of herself as a child, "I thought it no sin to
learn or hear witty songs and amorous sonnets or poems,
and twenty things of that kind, wherein I was so apt that I
became the confidant in all the loves that were managed
among my mother's young women."[37] These sonnets or
poems were not of Puritan origin, yet they were shared and
sung in a Puritan household; as a grown woman, she disapproves of them, yet her own description shows that when
she seeks to express her love of her husband, she still favors
that amorous style learned in her youth.[38]

Not all Puritans emphasize the sexual and sensual delight
of marital love. William Perkins does not make much of it.
He does say that "the Communion of man and wife" is a
duty which "consisteth principally in the performance of
speciall benevolence one to another, and that not of courte-
sie, but of due debt." Spouses must show "a singular and en-
tire affection one towards another," among other ways, "by
an holy kind of rejoycing and solacing themselves with each
other, in a mutuall declaration of the signes and tokens of
love and kindness." To support his position, he quotes not
only Proverbs 5.18–19, but also Song of Songs 1.1: "*Let him
kisse mee with the kisses of his mouth, for thy love is better*

then wine." On the other hand, Perkins does not say anything of this joyous and sensuous intimacy in his discussion
of the ends of marriage, though he does say that mutual
comfort is such end.[39]

Baxter, too, fails to make much of the sensual and sexual
side of marriage. He does tell husband and wife that they
must take delight in each other; he adds that men are perverse enough to turn "the *lawful delight* allowed them by
God . . . into loathing and disdain." This they must not do;
Proverbs 5.18–19 must be their guide.[40] Yet he does not
consider the mutual delights and comforts of marriage a
chief reason to marry. We must marry if we can serve God
and ourselves better by doing so, if our parents require it of
us (and there is *"no greater matter* on the contrary to hinder
it"), and if we are free to do so and "have not the gift of *Con-
tinence."* The good of mutual support and comfort comes in
by the back door, in answer to the question, *"May the aged
marry that are frigid, impotent, and uncapable of procreation? Answ.* Yes, God hath not forbidden them: And there
are other lawful ends of marriage, as mutual help and comfort *&c.* which may make it lawful."[41] It takes a question
about the aged to make him mention comfort as a reason for
marriage; he does not think that the old are that interested
in sexual delight. He quotes Bacon, who says that wives are
"old mens nurses"—a good enough reason for an elderly
man to marry. Baxter is less willing than others to integrate
the sexual with the affective, ethical, and even spiritual elements of marriage.[42] The character of Baxter's thought and
feeling perhaps misled Weber in his judgment of Puritanism,
for he takes Baxter as an exemplar of Puritan attitudes toward marital sexuality. Weber writes that the Song of Songs
"was for the most part simply ignored by the Puritans," but
in fact Puritan writers often turned to the Song of Songs to
illustrate the love that a husband must have for a wife, and a
wife for a husband, as the Hallers have noted.[43] In the main,
the Puritan treatments of marriage from the 1620s to the
1660s celebrated the carnality of conjugal life as Baxter
never did.

Modern dissociations of sexuality from the deeper dimensions of emotional life would not have been congenial to the Puritan sensibility. Writing of his own time, Weber remarks that "in a lecture, a zealous adherent of hygienic prostitution—it was a question of the regulation of brothels and prostitutes—defined the moral legitimacy of extra-marital intercourse (which was looked upon as hygienically useful) by referring to its poetic justification in the case of Faust and Margaret." He comments that treating Margaret as a prostitute and failing to distinguish "the powerful sway of human passion from sexual intercourse for hygienic reasons" is thoroughly Puritan.[44] Weber is mistaken; the Puritans understood and even sanctified the passionate desire and erotic longing for another which endowed the Puritan marriage bed with life-meanings far deeper than those captured by physiology. In marital love, with its sexuality, we find a true friend and companion, a second self: we are redeemed from our loneliness. The Puritans would have condemned the love that joined Gretchen and Faust together, but they call for a love within marriage no less deep or passionate.[45]

But marriage is by no means just a sensual relation for the Puritans. They believe that spouses must also be spiritually devoted to each other. Baxter tells us: *"A principal duty between husband and wife, is, With special care, and skill, and diligence, to help each other in the knowledge, and worship, and obedience of God, in order to their salvation."*[46] This, too, is an obligation which falls upon both husband and wife. Wives as well as husbands may criticize their spouses' thoughts, feelings, and actions out of a concern for their spiritual and moral well-being. Wives who are normally required to be docile and submissive thus have a certain freedom to be openly critical of their husbands—in the service (or apparent service) of God, of course.

Baxter urges husbands and wives to pray together in private, as well as with the larger family, which includes children and servants.[47] Gouge makes conjugal prayer one of the duties of marriage. He tells us that the need for "a true, spirituall, matrimoniall love" between husband and wife is one of the things "most meet to be mentioned in private prayer betwixt" them; spouses should pray "[t]hat such needfull gifts and graces as are wanting in either of them may be wrought: and such vices and infirmities as they are subject unto may be redressed."[48]

Such prayer between husband and wife provided one private occasion where wives could openly criticize their husbands. We need not simply assume that they did so; Baxter tells us, with startling frankness, that his late wife

> was very desirous that we should all have lived in a constancy of Devotion, and a blameless Innocency: And in this respect she was the meetest helper that I could have had in the world (the ever I was acquainted with): For I was apt to be over-careless in my Speech, and too backward in my Duty; And [at her death] she was still endeavouring to bring me to greater wariness and strictness in both: If I spake rashly or sharply, it offended her: If I carried it (as I was apt) with too much neglect of Ceremony, or humble Complement to any, she would modestly tell me of it: If my very Looks seemed not pleasant, she would have me amend them (which my weak pained state of Body undisposed me to do:) If I forgat any Week to Cathechise my Servants, and familiarly instruct them personally (besides my ordinary Family-Duties) she was troubled at my remissness. And whereas of late years my decay of Spirits, and deseased heaviness and pain, made me much more seldom and cold in profitable Conference and Discourse in my house, then I had been when I was younger, and had more Ease, and Spirits, and natural Vigour, she much blamed me, and was troubled at it, as a wrong to her self and others: . . . [though] of late years, my constant weakness and pain . . . [kept me much in] my Bed, that I was seldomer in secret Prayer with my Wife than she desired.[49]

This freedom of wives to criticize their husbands creates a tension within the Puritan marriage, for the Puritans are firmly convinced that men must rule and wives must obey. Gataker approvingly quotes Colossians 3.18: *"Wives, submit your selves unto your Husbands, as it is comely in the Lord."*[50] When thinking along these lines, the Puritans call for restraint in feeling as well as submission in action. Women must restrain their expressions of anger and discontent, even if their husbands' conduct gives them good grounds. Docility and a loving gentleness toward husbands are prime wifely virtues. This wifely restraint was to be balanced, according to the theorists of marriage, by husbands' gentle and restrained use of their own authority.[51]

Life is not all authority and submission; the Puritans knew that they lived in a material world of food and drink, bedstead and fireplace. Husband and wife must also care for each other's material and worldly comfort. Men who do not care for the physical well-being of their wives are severely condemned; prudence in managing household affairs is one of the chief virtues of a wife.[52] Gataker writes:

> It is no shame or staine . . . for a woman to be house-wifely, be she never so well borne, be she never so wealthy. For it is the *womans trade* so to be: it is the end of her *creation;* it is that that she was made for. She was made for man, and given to man, not to be a *play-fellow,* or *a bed-fellow,* or *a table-mate,* onely with him, (and yet to be all these too,) but to be *a yoake-fellow, a worke-fellow, a fellow-labourer* with him, to be *an assistant* and *an helper* unto him, in the managing of such *domesticall and household affaires.*[53]

Thus the prospect that a woman is prudent ought to weigh heavily when a man is choosing a mate. The wives of several eminent ministers in England and New England handled all the financial affairs of the family, leaving their husbands with greater liberty to concern themselves with matters spiritual and ecclesiastical. The men gave high praise to their women for this.[54]

Some writers put this obligation to care for the ethical, religious, and worldly well-being of one's spouse in words that recall Aristotle and Thomas. They say that husband and wife must be the best of friends; one may have no greater friend than one's spouse. Taylor, who was no Puritan but whose attitudes toward marriage were in many respects compatible with those of the Puritan casuists and theologians, asks "whether a friend may be more than a Husband or Wife." He answers that

> it can never be reasonable or just, prudent or lawful; but the reason is, because marriage is the Queen of friendships, in which there is a communication of all that can be communicated by friendship . . . other friendships are a part of this [marital friendship], they are marriages too, less indeed then the other, because they cannot, must not, be all the indearment which the other is; yet that being the principal, is the measure of the rest, and all to be honoured by like dignities, and measured by the same rules, . . . friendships are *Marriages* of the soul, and of fortunes and interests, and counsels . . . [as] they are *brotherhoods* too.[55]

It is useful to contrast this view of marriage as friendship with that of Cicero in the classical period. The Puritans were familiar with Cicero's *De Amicitia* as well as Aristotle's *Ethics*, but they were closer to Aristotle on this matter. Cicero believes that friendship can occur only among men. He finds much of the meaning of friendship in politics and war, although he thinks it can be enjoyed by those who have honorably retired from these worlds. By their own example, friends must encourage each other to act honorably in these harsh realms. We can love virtuous men "whom we have never seen," says Cicero. "Now, if the force of integrity is so great that we love it . . . in those we have never seen, . . . what wonder that men's souls are stirred when they think they see clearly the virtue and goodness of those with whom a close intimacy is possible?"[56]

Cicero offers Gaius Luscinus Fabricius, the Roman general and consul of the early third century B.C., as an example of a man whom he and his contemporaries have never seen and yet love. The general was considered by later Romans to be a model of the integrity and simplicity which marked the mores of earlier days. As the tale is told, Fabricius resisted attempts to be bribed; thus, in spite of his high offices, he died a poor man. Provision had to be made for his daughter out of funds of the state.

Women such as Fabricius' daughter could suffer or enjoy a fate created by the virtue of fathers and husbands in politics and war, but they were not, for Cicero, ordinarily active participants in these realms; they were not the stuff of which friends were made. Cicero held to the notion that women were by nature weak and light-minded (*infirmitas sexus* and *levitas animi*), although his first wife, Terentia, was quite the opposite. In his own time, some aristocratic women did take an active part in Roman political life, but for Cicero none were models of political virtue. He retained his admiration for the manners and morals of the early Romans, who, with some exceptions, reserved the worlds of politics and war for men.

For Cicero, eros prevents wives and husbands from being true friends. Although friendship means devotion and a delight in being together, it is not an erotic relation, or one in which eros is welcome. He disapproves of the homosexual friendships of Greek culture to which some Romans of his own time were drawn. Homosexual intercourse is unnatural, says Cicero. He cites the Roman poet Ennius, who writes: "Shame's beginning is the stripping of men's bodies openly."[57] Cicero agrees: the shameful practice of homosexual friendship had its origin, he thinks, "in the Greek gymnasia."[58]

In general he suspects sexuality, including the love of a man for a woman, "to which nature has granted wider tolerance" than it has to male homosexuality. In sexual pleasure and sexual longing, we lose the temperate, peaceful, and equable mood which the wise man seeks to have at all times.[59] He condemns Aristotle and the Peripatetics, who say that there is a proper place in our life for the agitated movement of our soul if that movement is not excessive. This view, he says, "must be regarded as weak and effeminate," *mollis et enervata.* "Those who are transported with delight at the enjoyment of sexual pleasures are degraded," he writes; "those who covet them with feverish soul are criminal. In fact the whole passion ordinarily termed love *[amor]* . . . is of such exceeding triviality that I see nothing that I think comparable with it."[60] *Amor* is worse than trivial, for it leads to foolish and dishonorable actions.

In their conception of married love, the Puritans reject Cicero's attitude toward women, friendship, and sexuality. Husband and wife must be the best of friends; sensuality and sexuality are integral parts of this friendship. The unselfish devotion men were to have for each other in the Ciceronian tradition has to give way not to a new world of unqualified egoism toward all, but to a sort of friendship with one's wife that was never called for by the Roman senator.

In this notion of marital love, many of the themes of classical and medieval texts on friendship, including some of Cicero's, are retained or given different form. The Puritans do not think that a major element of the friendship between husband and wife is the mutual encouragement to honorable action in politics and war, yet they do conceive of marital friendship as one which should ethically and spiritually nourish husband and wife, whatever their callings. Husbands and wives are joined in practical affairs, if not in matters of state.

Then again, while Cicero does not make the usefulness of friends in practical matters the fundamental principle of friendship, he does give it a place: true friends will help in politics and business if they can. Cicero thinks friends must nourish each other in the realm of letters, manners, conversation, and thought—in short, in the realm of urbane culture.[61] The Puritans do not think that marriage has this purpose (nor, for that matter, does Cicero, which may be one more reason why marriage does not fit into his conception of friendship).

The Puritans also bring some startling new notions to the

idea of marital friendship. The same Puritans who believe that husband and wife should concern themselves with the ethical and spiritual character of their spouse also believe that one of the greatest goods of life is being loved by one's spouse. The love itself is comforting: someone cares, takes delight. One is no longer alone in the world. This idea is a foundation of the Puritan theory of marriage.

The same idea is found in Taylor's thought. Objecting to the exalted belief that one should love a friend only for his virtue and not for what one hopes to receive from him, Taylor writes, "[A]lthough I love my friend because he is worthy, yet he is not worthy if he can do no good." What kind of good? "He only is fit to be chosen for a friend who can give counsel, or defend my cause, or guide me right, or relieve my need, or can and will, when I need it, do me good: only this I add: into the heaps of doing good, I will reckon" loving me, "for it is a pleasure to be beloved."[62]

Marriage is the model of all other human friendships. In no other relation with a man or woman can one be loved so well.

In examining Puritan ideas of marriage as part of the history of friendship, both in idea and in practice, one should not ignore Montaigne, who shares much with Cicero. He writes that as far as friendship goes, none of "the four ancient forms of association—natural, social, hospitable, erotic—come up to real friendship, either separately, or together." The love of woman "is more active, more scorching, and more intense" than that of true friendship. "But it is an impetuous and fickle flame, undulating and variable, a fever flame, subject to fits and lulls, that holds us only by one corner. In friendship it is a general and universal warmth, moderate and even, besides, a constant and settled warmth, all gentleness and smoothness, with nothing bitter and stinging about it."[63]

Montaigne thinks that the logics of desire in friendship and in our love of women are quite different. Adopting the view characteristic of the Roman poet Martial, Montaigne believes that a man's full possession of a woman destroys

his desire for her: "la jouyssance le perd"; he becomes sati-
ated, uninterested.[64] Friendship is different; the more it is
enjoyed, the more it is desired. The pleasure of a woman's
friendship must thus deprive a man of his desire for her. To
the extent that he desires her, she must not be his—but
what is the pleasure of her friendship without his secure
knowledge of her love for him?

And what of marriage, which is supposed to be a stable relation? A man cannot even hope that he and his wife will be
friends, for friendship must be freely given, while marriage
"is a bargain to which only the entrance is free—its contin-
uance being constrained and forced, depending otherwise
than on our will—and a bargain ordinarily made for other
ends." Montaigne adds that women are not ordinarily suited
for friendship. They commonly lack the "capacity" (perhaps
he means the powers of spirit and mind) which sustain the
"communion and fellowship" of friendship; "nor does their
soul seem firm enough to endure the strain of so tight and
durable a knot."[65] Is it then surprising that the same Montaigne who devotes a remarkable essay to the memory of his
friend Etienne de la Boétie, makes little mention of his wife?
The distance between Montaigne and the Puritans is great; I
need only mention the extraordinary records of conjugal
devotion left by Baxter in his memoir of his wife and by
Hutchinson in her memoir of her husband.[66]

Benjamin Nelson, in his outstanding essay on the history
of friendship in the West, says that the older ideal of an unselfish devotion of a man to his friend gave way, in early
modern Europe, to a new view, unsympathetic to this devotion. He believes that this shift in attitude is part of a larger
passage in the West from the older world views of "tribal
brotherhood" to the newer one of "universal otherhood."[67]
The older idea of friendship, in which devotion was only to
one or a few, did not become a basis for a new and triumphal
view in which devotion was to be given to ever wider human groups. It was not successfully universalized. Instead,
the idea of friendship came under attack and was ultimately

replaced by an ethic which emphasized the disciplined pursuit of personal good.

The belief that a man should stand surety for a friend in need, even at the risk of all his wealth, is often part of medieval and Renaissance ideas of friendship. We find it dramatically and profoundly developed in Shakespeare's *Merchant of Venice*. Nelson describes sixteenth-century attacks on this expression of unlimited devotion to a friend, the most striking of which is Luther's: "Standing surety is a work that is too lofty for a man; it is unseemly, for it is presumptuous and an invasion of God's rights. For . . . the Scriptures bid us to put our trust and place our reliance on no man, but only on God; for human nature is false, vain, deceitful, and unreliable."[68] In this matter, Luther finds an ally in Sir Walter Raleigh, who advises his son to

> suffer not thyself to be wounded for other men's faults, and scourged for other men's offences, which is the surety for another; for thereby millions of men have been beggared and destroyed, paying the reckoning of other men's riot, and the charge of other men's folly and prodigality; if thou smart, smart for thine own sins; and, above all things, be not made an ass to carry the burdens of other men: if any friend desire thee to be his surety, give him a part of what thou hast to spare; if he press thee further, he is not thy friend at all.[69]

Nelson may be right to think that within the realm of commerce in Reformation Europe, the belief that friends should be devoted to one another without limit gave way to the belief that they should at all times be governed by principles of rational business practice, making no exceptions on grounds of love or affection. The harshness of the world of commerce is not tempered by the notion that man should be a friend to man.

It is sad that the aristocratic idea of friendship among males did not extend to become a norm governing all human relations, among all human beings in all spheres of life. The claims of friendship in the seventeenth century did not disappear from the world, however. Indeed, in the sphere of marriage these claims became more powerful than they had ever been. In economic life, tribal brotherhood may have given way to universal otherhood, but in the realm of marriage, the belief in brotherhood and friendship moved forward. The idea of friendship among males was transformed into the love between husband and wife. The claims of friendship remained circumscribed in their application, "tribal," but they made their home, and still do, in one of the most common relations of modern life. The world of commerce lost some of the restraints that might have mitigated its harshness, but the world of marriage gained an ethic which, if heeded at all, made it more humane.

In a later essay, Nelson takes account of some of these developments: "Too few seem to perceive that in the medieval world and in the early modern world—prior, actually, to the Puritans—a full religious sacralization of the family or of family property did not exist. There did, indeed, not occur the sacralization of what might be called the special friendship with one's own wife." He interprets the Puritan call for friendship with one's spouse, however, in a curious way: it is "the sacralization of a collective egoism of the family and its property." It is thus far from the ideal of male friendship in antiquity and the middle ages, which Nelson says "was conceived as the union that transcended all calculations and egotism whether of family or of person. From at least the time of Plato forward, the moralists and novelists insisted on preeminence of friendship, going so far as to deny that one's wife or members of one's family could truly be friends in the highest sense."[70]

This is a prejudiced reading of friendship's twists and turns in history. Puritan marital love is no more a collective egoism than is the friendship among virtuous men espoused by Cicero. Cicero calls for a collective egoism among friends to the extent that friends ought to favor each other over others, but this alliance has its limits; friends must not ask each other to do what is shameful, for they must be exemplars of virtue to one another.[71]

The union of man and wife in Puritan thought is no less ethical. The Puritan writers believed that a chief end, or *the* chief end, of marriage is mutual support and comfort; that sexual and sensual delight is essential to that comfort; that husband and wife must also be the best of friends; and that this delight and friendship must last, neither may wane with the years.

In view of these ideas, Weber's belief that the "decisive characteristic" of the Puritans was their asceticism which turned all its force against the spontaneous enjoyment of life, must be rejected.[72] The Puritan ethic of marriage is genuinely world-affirming. The love and desire that a husband and wife bear for each other are intrinsically good things which bring delight to the world. One cannot agree that, to the Puritans, "everything pertaining to the flesh" was corrupt.[73] Far from it! To a remarkable degree, the flesh is given an honored place.

The evidence provided by the Puritan minister-writers refutes the belief that the Puritans were thoroughly hostile to the personal and emotional dependence of one adult upon another. Weber writes that Puritanism expresses a "disillusioned and pessimistically inclined individualism," a distrust of others which comes out in "warnings against any trust in the aid of friendship of men. . . . Every purely emotional, that is not rationally motivated, personal relation of man to man easily fell in the Puritan, as in every ascetic ethic, under the suspicion of idolatry of the flesh." In Weber's view of Puritanism, "Only God should be your confidant."[74]

While it is true that in their hostility to the ideal of male friendship, the Puritans counseled against a great trust of a man in other men, they also called for a marriage in which spouses could trust and depend upon one another to a high degree. The Puritan man or woman was not meant to be— or to feel—alone in the world; God made marriage and the two sexes so that man would not be alone.

Nor was he meant to be alone in his relations with God. The evidence does not support Weber's belief that the Puritan's "intercourse with his God" was meant to be "carried on in deep spiritual isolation."[75] It is true, as Weber notes, that John Bunyan has his pilgrim leave his wife and children when they hold him back from his voyage to salvation, but this is no evidence of the "inner isolation of the individual" in Puritanism.[76] A concern for the state of his soul *did* come first for the Puritan. He could not let his family draw him from this. But in a proper marriage, husband and wife are companions in a quest for holiness and salvation.

This critique of Weber's views also disproves some of his most interesting theories about the links of Puritanism to that which preceded and followed it. Looking backward, Weber sees a continuity between Western monasticism and the Puritan ethic. The monastic rejected the pleasures of the world and served God in systematically self-disciplined fashion, attempting to mold heart, mind, desire, and intention to a single purpose. The Puritan tried to do the same, but in the world rather than behind monastic walls.[77] In Puritanism, the Christian asceticism of the monastery "strode into the market place of life, slammed the door of the monastery behind it, and undertook to penetrate . . . [the] daily routine of life with its methodicalness, to fashion it into a life in the world, but neither of nor for this world."[78]

If Weber was correct in his belief that the mainstream of Western monasticism sought by methodical means to form constant motives and a permanent order within the heart of the monk and the nun, then he detected a noteworthy continuity between monasticism and Puritanism. But if the monastic spirit was also as ascetic and world-rejecting as Weber said it was, then the Puritan is not only different from the monk by being *in* the world, but by being (with respect to marriage, at least) *of* and *for* the world. Erasmus and the Christian humanists, with their attack on celibacy and their support of marriage, broke with the world-rejecting ethic of monasticism. In their views on marriage, both the humanists and the Puritans asserted that the world was good.

Although the Puritans affirmed the carnal or worldly element of marital love, they did not mean to leave the natural erotic desires of humanity untouched. The erotic attachment and delight of the "natural" man had to be made steady and reliable. By systematic self-discipline, the changeability of natural desire was transformed into something more constant and steady. "Put case," writes Rogers, that "thou hadst grounds of first love to thy companion: what then? thinkst though that this edge will holde without dayly whetting?"[79]

The Puritans understood, however, that there was something beyond reason's control in marital love. It is as mysterious, writes Rogers, as the

> league of friendship, wherein we see God doth so order it, that by a secret instinct of love and sympathy, causing the heart of one to incline to the other, two friends have beene knit so close to the other, that they have beene as one spirit in two bodies, as not only wee see in *Jonathan* and *David*, but in heathens which have striven to lay downe their lives for the safeguard of each other. . . . [O]ftimes a reason cannot be given by either partie, why they should be so tender each to other: It being caused not by any profitable or pleasurable meane, but by meere sympathy, which is farre the more pure and noble cement of union, than what else so ever.[80]

There is a similar mystery at the heart of marital love. Its causes are largely hidden and unknown, and hence beyond our control. "[T]he elme and the vine doe naturally so entwine and embrace each the other, that its called, the friendly elme; who can tell why? much more then in reasonable creatures, it must be so." Rogers even celebrates marital love's distance from the dictates of cool judgment: "[T]hrough this instinct of sympathie . . . two consent together to become husband and wife," setting all others aside, although they are "more amiable in themselves, more rich, better bred, and the like."[81]

Other writers do not go quite this far, but agree that love is rooted in temperamental affinities which we cannot rule.[82] If we are wrongly joined, happiness is beyond our reach. Puritan casuists therefore counsel their readers to make a very careful choice of partner. To marry, they say, it is not necessary to be deeply in love, but a real likelihood that such love will develop is necessary. No one ought to marry a person he thinks he cannot or is not likely to love. This sense of one's affinity for a proposed spouse is of greater importance than the wishes of one's own parents, weighty as those may be.[83]

Temperament is basic, but it is not all. Spouses can cultivate their delight in each other. To help couples keep the edge on their marital love, Puritan writers offer practical advice. Gouge, for example, tells us that "outward mutual peace" is "one of the principall . . . means of maintaining an inward loving affection betwixt Man and Wife." They should therefore "avoid offence"; if it is given, they should pass it by. "Let them suffer their own will to be crossed, rather than discontent be given to the other." If both be incensed together, "offer reconciliation"; if reconciliation is offered, accept it. Do not bring "children, servants," or others "in the family" into your frays. Do not compare your spouse to another. "Bee not jealous. . . . Endeavour to please one another."[84] Counseling husbands, Baxter says, "Make not the infirmities" of your wives "to seem *odious faults*, but excuse them as far as you lawfully may, by considering the frailty of the Sex . . . and considering also your *own* infirmities, and how much your *Wives* must bear with you."[85]

The Puritans valued constancy of motive and purpose in all areas of life; indeed, it was essential to the personality type they called for. But the constancy and self-control required of Puritans was not intrinsically linked to either world-affirming or world-rejecting attitudes. In marriage, a steady and reliable delight in one's spouse was called for just as much as a constant and thorough restraint in the use and enjoyment of wealth. While there were distinctly ascetic elements in the mainstream of Puritan ethics—a restraint in consumption, "especially of luxuries," and a rejection of all "superfluities" and "vain ostentation" among them—the evidence makes it clear that a rejection of the world and its delights was not "the final decisive religious motive" of Puritanism.[86]

The Puritan ethic of constancy was not intrinsically opposed to the world, but it was opposed to the polyvalent character of human feeling. A "law of ambivalence," writes Freud in his "Reflections upon War and Death," "governs our emotional relations with those we love most. . . . Loved ones are on the one hand an inner possession, an ingredient of our personal ego, but on the other hand are partly strangers, even enemies. With the exception of only a very few situations, there adheres to the tenderest and closest of our affections a vestige of hostility."[87] The ethic of constancy restrained the negative pole of this amibivalence in marriage. Hostile or aggressive feelings toward one's spouse were to be minimized and their direct expression severely restricted. But constancy also provided a well-used route for dealing with these unwanted feelings. The constant and thorough concern which devout Puritans characteristically showed toward their spouses can be seen as a reaction-formation against the pressure of hostile and aggressive impulses. Their conduct had the meticulous and anxious character of obsessive behavior, suggesting that the origins of ethical constancy lie in something repressed—undoubtedly these unwanted negative feelings. Thus the ethic of constancy not only created a problem for husbands and wives by opposing a natural tendency toward polyvalent feelings, it also provided the solution. Devoted adherence to the ethic itself offered a means by which spouses could sublimate their unwanted feelings. From the point of view of the ethic of constancy, this was a highly desirable solution, for it gave the energy of the unwanted feelings over to the ethic itself.

But it was not a solution designed to make men and women altogether happy. The Puritan demand for constancy in all areas of life, wrote Weber, generally required "the destruction of spontaneous, impulsive enjoyment."[88] This is certainly the way it appears from a twentieth-century vantage point. But Weber's statement should not be taken as a description of what the Puritans themselves sought. They did not think that the demand for constancy was a necessary enemy of spontaneity, much less of erotic delight. In the case of married life, the Puritans called for an integration of all these elements.[89] On the other hand, Weber's judgment might be taken as a description of the psychology actually created by the demand for constancy. There is good reason to think that the severe restraints the Puritans put upon the development and expression of hostile or aggressive feelings severely limited the possibilities of erotic excitement for many men and women.

"The spontaneous vitality of impulsive action" which Weber saw threatened by constancy was not the spontaneity of moderate emotions, of calm and easy pleasures, of sweet and gentle joy. It was the spontaneity of passion and intense and agitated excitement.[90] Sexual desire, love, and attraction do of course contribute some of the energy required for such excitement. But they are often insufficient in themselves to provide the intensity and length of passionate agitation which people desire. According to Robert Stoller, the expression and elaboration of aggression or hostility—as supplementary elements—are two of the most characteristic ways in which people achieve the amount and length of excitement they desire.[91] The Puritan ethic denied spouses this route to satisfaction. It did so not simply by restraining the expression of aggression and anger, but by converting their energy to its own purposes. It therefore depended upon its restraints against aggression for its own survival. Thus it is not surprising, despite the world-affirming ideal of the Puritan marriage, that Weber sees the Puritan ethic as hostile to the pleasures of erotic excitement.

Before considering the negative ramifications of the Puritan's self-imposed plight, however, let us pursue its most positive aspect, the integrative impulse, as explored in the dramatic literature of the ensuing period.

5

Passion, Fidelity, and the Stage

The compatibility of passion and fidelity was a subject of public debate two centuries before Weber. The downfall of the Puritan regime permitted the reopening of the London stage, and it was on this stage, rather than in texts of moral philosophy or theology, that the Puritan demand for both constancy and mutual delight was debated. In comedies whose central subject was courtship and marriage, playwrights of the period attempted to develop the idea of integration. Although they offered fantastic resolutions rather than practical solutions to the conflict between constancy and spontaneity, these writers suggest that integration is not entirely implausible.

The premise of many of these comedies was that the elaboration of excitement between a man and a woman who find themselves sexually attracted to one another is available only outside of marriage. The trouble with marriage, they say, is that it is boring, particularly for men. In Dryden's *Marriage a-la-Mode* [1672],[1] Rodophil complains that two years of married life has destroyed the great passion he once had for his wife, Doralice. Familiarity has bred disinterest. As the novelty has faded, so has the excitement. Rodophil admits that his wife has many good qualities: she is young, is said to be a great beauty, and her humor suits him well, for it is very much like his own.

But he can no longer tell even whether she is a great beauty or not: "Ask those," he comments, "who have smelt to a strong perfume two years together, what's the scent" (I.i.154–55). If Rodophil could parcel Doralice's virtue out to three or four women, and if he could sleep with them all, then he would not become bored; but he must always be with *her*. She excites him so little that he can no longer even satisfy her. Because husbands "cannot feed on one dish," she laments, wives "must be starv'd" (III.i.101–02). He tells her he has tried to deal with the problem, but the old tricks no longer work:

> I have taken such pains to enjoy thee, *Doralice*,
> that I have fanci'd thee all the fine women in
> the Town, to help me out. But now there's none left
> for me to think on, my imagination is quite jaded.
> Thou are a Wife, and thou wilt be a Wife, and I
> can make thee another no longer. (III.i.89–94)[2]

Novelty and mystery are difficult but not impossible to find in marriage. Discovering that a friend wants to sleep with Doralice, Rodophil concludes that there must be something in his wife that he has not seen, "some rich Mine, for ought I know, that I have not yet discover'd" (V.i.367–68). This possibility alleviates the boredom for a while.

Perhaps if wives could remain unseen, he surmises, they might retain their allure, for then men could project whatever face and body they desired upon them; reality impedes men's imagination. Masked women fare better than wives in satisfying men's desire.[3] In Dryden's *Secret Love* [1667], Florimell and Celadon meet. She is masked. He complains (in jest):

> Now I am sure I have the worst on't: for you see the
> worst of me, and that I do not of you till you shew
> your face:———
> Yet now I think on't, you must be handsome.———

FLORIMELL.   What kind of beauty do you like?

CELADON.   Just such a one as yours.

FLORIMELL.   What's that?

CELADON.   Such an Ovall face, clear skin, hazle eyes,
thick brown Eye-browes, and Hair as you have for all
the world. . . . [T]hen you have,———let me see.

FLORIMELL.   I'll swear you shan'not see.———

CELADON.   A turn'd up Nose: that gives an air to your
face: Oh, I find I am more and more in love with you!
a full neather-lip, an out-mouth, that makes mine
water at it: the bottom of your cheeks a little blub,
and two dimples when you smile: for your stature,
'tis well, and for your wit 'twas given you by one that
knew it had been thrown away upon an ill face;
come you are handsome, there's no denying it.
(I.i.109–18, 123–33)

Florimell responds that Celadon's interest stems from igno-
rance. (But save for the turned-up nose, Celadon accurately
describes Nell Gwynn, one of the brightest stars of the late-
seventeenth-century stage, and the Florimell of the original
production.)[4]

The challenge of the chase, with the prospect of a satisfying capture, brings life to men's desire, but that excitement is lost once the capture is actually made.[5] Courtship
may be interesting, but marriage is not. Vainlove, in Congreve's *The Old Batchelour* [1693], loses interest in women
as soon as they give in to his desires. Thus, a paradox arises:
How can Araminta marry Vainlove if she would drive him
away by saying yes? When he finally proposes, she can do
nothing but put him off: "O my Conscience," comments a
friend, "she dares not consent, for fear he shou'd recant"
(V.ii.175–76).

If serious commitment means the death of desire, men
must not be too serious about fidelity. Celadon courts Florimell by making much of his inconstancy: "[G]ive me some
Twenty, some Forty, some a Hundred Mistresses, I have
more Love than any one woman can turn her to." Let her

not think him unreasonable, however: "I can live with as few Mistresses as any man: I desire no superfluities; onely for necessary change or so; as I shift my Linnen." Florimell responds in kind. He should not worry about leaving her; were he to stay around, he would deny her the pleasure of a new and fresher man (*Secret Love* I.i.73–90).[6] Lacking the male psychology, what can she do in defense but adopt it? Although it is not natural to her, the style appeals to men like Celadon.

He is not kidding, either, about his unfaithfulness. While in love with Florimell, he still chases two belles of the court whom he loves much less. He cannot give up the sweetness of "variety." "Well," he says, "we must all sin, and we must all repent, and there's an end on't" (III.i.427–30). Apparently, masculine inconstancy is better suited to the Roman Catholic cycle of sin, guilt, and repentance than it is to the Puritan conscience.

Given the male psyche, these women characters would be fools to take male confessions of love at face value. However sincere these men believe themselves to be, the conditions for their own sexual excitement give the lie to their words. Since men understand this, women's suspicions are taken by them as a recognition of their masculinity. As long as female skepticism doesn't incorporate actual dislike, men enjoy it.

In Shadwell's *Bury-fair* [1689], Wildish courts Gertrude in elevated language:

> Your Eyes strike every one you level at, like Lightning through a Cloud.
> GERTRUDE.   Very pretty! Shall I oblige Mr. *Trim* [a fatuous fop] with this fine expression? he'll give you any money for it. (II.i)

Bellamy, the rival of Wildish, does not fare better:

> BELLAMY.   . . . Wou'd you cou'd see the Wounds you make in Hearts; then, Madam, mine wou'd expect your pity.

GERTRUDE. This is a very pretty Scene; runs smoothly off the Tongue, and is very well Acted: Can you do it over again? (III.i)

Men like this hostility. As the Second Prologue of *Secret Love* says to the wits of the audience, "the little Hectors of the Pit,"

> You think your selves ill us'd
> When in smart Prologues you are not abus'd.
> A civil Prologue is approv'd by no man;
> You hate it as you do a Civil Woman:
> Your Fancy's pall'd, and liberally you pay
> To have it quicken'd, e're you see a Play.
> Just as old Sinners worn from their delight,
> Give money to be whip'd to appetite. (17–24)

The stimulants of excitement so far described—novelty, mystery, variety, verbal sparring—combine in a style called wit. Why did lady and gallant find wit so sexy? Perhaps it was the double entendres.

In Charles Sedley's *The Mulberry Garden* [1668], Wildish proposes to Olivia, commenting that although he gives up his liberty, "Which is dearer than life,"

> there is no service so desperate, that a gallant man
> will shrink at, if he like his reward; and to give his
> hand thus to a woman, in him that rightly under-
> stands what he does, is as bold an action as *Mutius
> Scaevola*'s [who thrust his hand in the fire]: yet that
> I may use it hereafter where and when I plase, upon
> my dear Olivia I'le venture it.
> OLIVIA. Softly, when you please, and where I please.
> (V.iv.51–58)[7]

Such references to the details of sexual play only en-hanced the excitement already created by wit, which could make things lively without being bawdy.[8] The Puritans trans-formed the energies of aggression into constancy, reduc-ing excitement. Wit, however, builds upon the excitement of hostility. What makes wit exciting is the aggression expressed within it, elaborated through the use of art and intelligence, for aggression elegantly expressed is raised to the level of an aesthetic achievement. It is no longer uncouth.

The most admired form of wit was repartee, the sharp and humorous reply, as in the following duet from Dryden's *An Evening's Love* [1668]. The Englishman Wildblood is smitten by the Spaniard Jacinta as he observes her at prayer in the church. He introduces himself.

> WILDBLOOD.   Madam, I hope a stranger may take the libertie without offence to offer his devotions by you.
> JACINTA.   That, Sir, would interrupt mine, without being any advantage to your own.
> WILDBLOOD.   My advantage, Madam, is very evident; for the kind Saint to whom you pray, may by the neighbourhood mistake my devotions for yours.
> JACINTA.   O Sir! Our Saints can better distinguish between the prayers of a Catholick and a Lutheran.
> WILDBLOOD.   I beseech you, Madam, trouble not your self for my Religion; for though I am a Heretick to the men of your Country, to your Ladies I am a very zealous Catholick: and for fornication and adulterie, I assure you I hold with both Churches. (I.ii.51–64)

"As for repartie," says Dryden, "as it is the very soul of conversation, so it is the greatest grace of Comedy, where it is proper to the Characters: there may be much of acuteness in a thing well said; but there is more in a quick reply" (Dryden, preface to *An Evening's Love*, lines 162–66). "Wit always looks more graceful," Quintilian concurs, "in reply than in attack."[9]

In a traditional courtship, when a man and woman have only recently and happily discovered their love for one another, their negative feelings are often overshadowed by a passionate accentuation of their feelings of love and admiration. The interest of the late-seventeenth-century comedies of courtship lies in their attempt to bring into the play of

courtship the antagonism and hostility that inevitably surface in married life. They present an imaginative consideration of what life would be like if this antagonistic element
between lovers were allowed to find full expression before
marriage, while the lovers are still independent.

Neither witty lady nor witty gallant dares lose himself or
herself to devotion and thus to sacrifice the freedom to express both sides of the ambivalence. When Florimell responds to Celadon's profession of love by saying that he has
done her "the greatest pleasure in the world" (*Secret Love*
II.i.61–62),[10] she parodies ideas of seventeenth-century romance, doubting the sincerity of the words she hears and expressing the negative side of her feelings toward Celadon.
He is now completely at her mercy.

> FLORIMELL.   I would have a Lover, that if need be,
> should hang himself, drown himself, break his neck,
> and poyson himself for very despair: he that will
> scruple this is an impudent fellow if he says he is in
> love.
> CELADON.   Pray, Madam, which of these four things
> would you have your Lover do? for a man's but a
> man, he cannot hang, and drown, and break his neck,
> and poyson himself, all together.
> FLORIMELL.   Well then, because you are but a begin-
> ner, and I would not discourage you, any one of these
> shall serve your turn in a fair way. (II.i.77–83)[11]

How long can excitement survive without this freedom to
express both positive and negative feelings? If all the energy
of negative emotions is withdrawn from expression, what is
left to fuel excitement? Can positive affect alone, day in and
day out, do the job?

During a courtship, negative feelings can be expressed
through a desire to be free, inconstant, separate, and independent, just as positive feelings can be expressed through a
desire for union. The circumstances of courtship in late-
seventeenth-century comedy permit gallant and lady ample
scope for the expression of both emotions. Lovers meet as

free agents, owing each other nothing. In marriage, as the Puritans saw it, such freedom is lost.

Can there be a form of marriage which retains the spirit and freedom of courtship? In Roman comedy love triumphs when lovers marry, surmounting the obstacles posed by others; these plays raise no doubts about the future of their protagonists. In English comedy of the late seventeenth century, the same thing often occurs even when the obstacles to marriage come from within the lovers' own hearts. But playwrights of the period occasionally explore the comic possibilities of life after the wedding, most successfully in scenes where gallant and lady agree to marry on terms which permit them to live as separate beings. With this arrangement, they hope the excitement and desire which bring them to marry will be sustained.[12]

Florimell asks Celadon how they should live once they are married, and he replies:

> As for the first year according to the laudable custome of new married people, we shall follow one another up into Chambers, and down into Gardens, and think we shall never have enough of one another.———So far 'tis pleasant enough I hope.
>
> FLORIMELL.   But after that, when we begin to live like Husband and Wife, and never come near one another———what then Sir?
>
> CELADON.   Why then our onely happiness must be to have one mind, and one will, *Florimell*.
>
> FLORIMELL.   One mind if thou wilt, but prithee let us have two wills, for I find one will be little enough for me alone. (*Secret Love* V.i.538–50)[13]

In true friendship, classical and medieval philosophers said, there is but one soul in two bodies; marriage, the Puritans, declared, is that union. Florimell and Celadon, however, think that marriage should not put an end to courtship; as Celadon says, "Whereas the names of Husband and Wife hold forth nothing, but clashing and cloying, and dullness and faintness in their signification; they shall be abol-

ish'd for ever betwixt us"; "we will be married," adds
Florimell, "by the more agreeable names of Mistress and
Gallant" (V.i.571–76).

The law and custom of late-seventeenth-century England required wifely obedience. Theologians—and not only
Puritan ones—called upon wives to make this command
part of their hearts and minds. How could this be seen as
anything but an attack upon a woman's separateness? In the
proviso scene of Congreve's *The Way of the World* [1700],
the gallant Mirabell asks Millamant,

> Have you any more Conditions to offer? Hitherto
> your demands are pretty reasonable.
> MILLAMANT.   Trifles,———As liberty to pay and re-
> ceive visits to and from whom I please, to write and
> receive Letters, without Interrogatories or wry Faces
> on your part. To wear what I please; and choose Con-
> versation with regard only to my own taste; to have
> no obligation upon me to converse with Wits that I
> don't like, because they are your acquaintance; or to
> be intimate with Fools, because they may be your
> Relations. Come to Dinner when I please, dine in my
> dressing room when I'm out of humour without giv-
> ing a reason. To have my Closet Inviolate; to be sole
> Empress of my Tea-table, which you must never pre-
> sume to approach without first asking leave. And
> lastly, where ever I am, you shall always knock at
> the door before you come in. These Articles sub-
> scrib'd, If I continue to endure you a little longer, I
> may by degrees dwindle into a Wife. (IV.i.210–27)

Upon first reading this passage, I thought that Congreve
was developing the idea that women as well as men have the
right to an independent life, even within marriage. This
seemed to me to be a fundamentally moral idea, based on
the belief that autonomy is an intrinsic good to which all
human beings have a right.[14] I now think that this reading
was mistaken. The autonomy Millamant desires is not for

its own sake, but for ultimately sexual purposes. It is the necessary condition for excitement.

The demand for excitement has strong moral implications, since it challenges the permanence and hierarchy of marriage. The husband's authority, so stressed by the Puritans, cannot fit into a marriage designed to provide excitement, for that requires a variety of women, or a woman whose wit and strength is her husband's match. "And dee hear," says Millamant,

> I won't be call'd Names.
> MIRABELL. Names!
> MILLAMANT. Ay as Wife, Spouse, My dear, Joy, Jewel, Love, Sweet heart and the rest of that Nauseous Cant, in which Men and their Wives are so fulsomely familiar,———I shall never bear that.
> (IV.i.194–200)

Dryden develops the comedy of penalty clauses. If Florimell violates his privileges, says Celadon, he won't have her in his bed for a month. To this she replies that if he violates her privileges, she'll give him horns. Equal in freedom, imagination, intelligence, and power to punish one another, they can look forward to an exciting life together. It is not as good as "wenching," Celadon tells Florimell, but it is, he admits, "very good" (V.i.586–88). Their common will to autonomy may be the one thing that will keep their marriage alive.

The comedies cited thus far achieve their wit by supposing that if mutual devotion is incompatible with excitement within marriage, then unity and hierarchy must give way. This argument apparently put the Puritan ethic of marriage on the defensive, since that ethic had called for both constancy and erotic delight. However, a reading of Shadwell's *Bury-fair*, which upholds the Puritan position, suggests that high excitement was not essential to marital delight. The premise of this play, like the earlier ones, is the incompatibility of excitement and constancy, but Shadwell's resolution is different. He concludes that the delight required in marriage is not heady excitement but steady enjoyment, and that enjoyment is compatible with constancy and the authority of the husband.

Throughout the first four acts of *Bury-fair*, Gertrude refuses the proposals of Lord Bellamy and his rival Wildish; she takes far too much joy in her freedom to think of parting with it (V.i). Wildish is excited by this independent streak,[15] but Bellamy is different. He is willing to give up excitement for mutual devotion and a union of souls in which he will be the higher power. When he discovers that his devoted young servant Charles is in fact Gertrude's sister Philadelphia in disguise (she has maintained the ruse to avoid marrying a man she does not love), he proposes marriage. In her pose as Charles, Philadelphia's devotion and youthful charm have delighted Bellamy. He had already vowed to remain with "him" for life, and had begun to treat "him" as a friend rather than a servant (I.ii). The submission and devotion Philadelphia exhibited as a servant leave Bellamy with no doubts about her suitability as a wife. "I was Passionate to Marry the other Sister, because I lov'd her; but I think it more reasonable to Marry this, because she loves me" (V.i).

Bellamy is not dismayed by his lack of passion for Philadelphia. Perhaps he would be if he expected a reliable excitement from his marriage. But Philadelphia as Charles did not sexually excite him, and now that he knows Charles is a young woman who can become his wife, he does not expect much more. He looks forward only to more of the same calm enjoyment he and Philadelphia have already shared.

The contrast between the delight of marriage (enjoyment) and the delight of amorous relations outside of marriage (excitement) is also made explicit in Vanbrugh's *The Relapse* [1696]. Loveless, returning to Amanda, the wife he had deserted, discovers for the first time the calm pleasures of home:

Through all the Roving Pleasures of my Youth,
. . . Where Nights and Days seemed all consum'd in
    Joy,

. . . .
I never knew one Moment's Peace like this.
Here . . . in this little soft Retreat,
My thoughts unbent from all the Cares of Life,

. . . .
The raging Flame of wild destructive Lust
Reduc'd to a warm pleasing Fire of lawful Love,
My Life glides on, and all is well within. (I.i)

But Loveless is not immune to the thrill of excitement—the greatest threat to male constancy—and he succumbs to it when he makes a visit to London. The city and its women take hold of him once again.

Because constancy was such a central concern of Puritan ethics, one might expect a general ethic favoring enjoyment over excitement to develop among the heirs of Puritanism. Such an ethic is in fact quite apparent in *Bury-fair*, where Shadwell develops an opposition between stability and excitement similar to that already found in classical Roman literature. In the play, Lord Bellamy resides in the country, enjoying the moderate and sober delights it offers to someone of his position. In younger days, Bellamy and Wildish shared the excitement of city life, and now Wildish wants him back. "Prethee, my Dear Peer, fling off this melancholy thought of Retirement, . . . what can be the diversion of a Country Life?" (III.i). Bellamy replies:

I view my stately Fields and Meads, laden with Corn and Grass; my Herds of Kine, and Flocks of Sheep; my Breed of Horses; my Delicate Gardens full of all sorts of Fruits and Herbs; my River full of Fish, with Ponds, and a Decoy for Water Fowl, and plenty of Game of all kinds in my Fields and Woods; my Parks for Venison; my Cellar well furnish'd with all variety of excellent Drinks: and all my own, *Ned*. (III.i)

The best England has to offer can be acquired with greater ease in London, Wildish rejoins. "But I have pleasure in reading the *Georgics*," answers Bellamy, "and contemplating the Works of Nature."

WILDISH.   I contemplate the chief Works of Nature:
fine Women; and the Juice of the Grape, well con-
cocted by the Sun. (III.i)

Wildish wants steady excitement. What the country can
offer, asserts Bellamy, is the peaceable enjoyment of what is
securely one's own. In the country, he says, he can count on
what is his: his herds, his horses, and so on. But "'[t]is . . .
the Country," replies Wildish; "a pretty Habitation for Birds
and Cattel: but Man is a herded Animal, and made for
Towns and Cities." How can a life be happy that sacrifices
itself to a fear of risk? "At our years," to leave "good Wine,
fine Women, Music, Wit and Sense, and true Pleasure!"
There's time enough for that "when we are weary of living"
(I.ii).

During the last forty years of the seventeenth century,
English playwrights engaged in what amounted to a systematic analysis—hardly superseded—of marriages devoted to
excitement or enjoyment. The inspiration to do so owed a
good deal to the Puritan theories, which had put such stress
on the fusion of constancy and delight. To evoke such spir-
ited responses, these theories must have had a good deal of
cultural power.

Yet their power was flawed. The mutual delight which
Puritans required of spouses was very likely the gentle and
moderate joy Bellamy and Philadelphia experience in Shadwell's play. Sexual excitement which drew upon both negative and positive poles of feeling for its strength (as exempli-
fied in Dryden and Congreve) was incompatible with the
constancy of feeling demanded by the Puritan ethic. It not
only threatened the emotional steadiness of the union between husband and wife, but authorized the elaboration of
aggressive and hostile feelings in women which were inappropriate to their place in the Puritan hierarchy. In spite of
its positive views of sexuality within marriage, it is understandable that Puritanism has acquired a bad name with respect to its attitude toward eroticism. The steady temper it
demanded was not conducive to passion.

6

Pamela and the
Hierarchy of the Sexes

It was widely held in medieval and Renaissance Europe that women were lustier than men, but the prominent Puritan theologians of the seventeenth century did not consider either sex notably more lusty than the other. Out of this neutral setting, a new hierarchy of sexuality was created in eighteenth-century England, in which men were seen as the lustier of the two sexes and women, weaker in their desire, were less subject to moral failure.

In strength, energy, drive, and forcefulness, in their will to mastery and command, and in their animal exuberance, men were taken to be naturally superior to women. But virility, in the Puritan's view, is amoral, and therefore masculinity is inherently defective. True men are like bulls: powerful, sexual, commanding, but lacking in conscience. Their will to power and their desire for animal pleasure leads them away from the paths of morality. Men's physical superiority to women therefore implies its complement, women's spiritual superiority to men. Women, naturally lacking in animality and the will to power, respond with less difficulty, more directly, more freely, to their own impulse to be good and to do right. Women possess a greater moral purity because their conscience occupies a more prominent (and less besieged) place in their bodies and minds. Their hearts vibrate in response to the moral demands of life.

Two ideas about women, prompted by the seventeenth-century Puritans but having their origin, I suspect, in the Christian humanism of the late-fifteenth and sixteenth centuries, paved the way for eighteenth-century Englishmen to give women exemplary moral status. The first was the Puritan belief that a wife has an obligation to concern herself with all the ethical dimensions of her husband's life (as described in chapter 4). Silence or disinterest over one's husband's ethics and character was no wifely virtue for the Puritans.

This idea was not peculiar to them; it could also be found in non-Puritan elements of the Church of England, in Roman Catholicism, and among other Protestants. But the wife's concern for her husband's ethical character assumed an importance in Puritan culture which it did not generally possess elsewhere due to the Puritan emphasis on the family as the fundamental ethical and religious unit. The family was to pray together; substantial ethical and religious instruction was to take place in the home; and the self-critical review of one's life and conduct was also to take place there. Regular confession of sins to a priest was not available to the devout Puritan. He needed a journal—and a wife. The consequence of this outlook was the more generally applicable idea that women's consciences had a moral stature equal to that of men's—even if women (by Biblical injunction) were to be subordinate to men in both public and private life. The eighteenth-century attitude toward women was built on this Puritan respect for women, but it transformed the idea of equality of the feminine conscience into a belief in feminine moral superiority. It asked more of women's consciences than it did of men's. The attitude therefore should not be called Puritan, for the mainstream of seventeenth-century Puritanism could not have accepted this feminization of conscience.

The other Puritan attitude which paved the way for a

woman's special place in the moral hierarchy has already been mentioned. It is best described as the *absence* of the older idea that women are the lustier of the two sexes. The rejection of this idea is probably a consequence of the Puritan belief, expressed in family practice, that women's consciences have a moral stature equal to that of men's. The change in Western attitudes toward the relative strength of sexuality in men and women may be attributed to changes in both the conception and the treatment of the moral capacities of women. When women are treated with less moral respect, they will be regarded as more subject to the demands of sexuality. In the medieval world, generally, they were regarded as inferior moral creatures and were therefore treated as the more lusty of the two sexes. The Puritans treated them as roughly equal in moral stature to men, and therefore generally made no distinction in terms of lustiness. By the eighteenth century, women had become the more moral of the two sexes, so their sexuality was considered to be weaker.

This transformation of ideas may be both a cause and a consequence of an actual change in the relative balance of repression. It may be that women were less moralized than men in medieval Europe; men had greater access than women to moralizing institutions. Denied access to universities and other conscience-forming institutions of the medieval world, women may have been less subject to the forces which created new and internalized sources of moral repression. Although women were still excluded from some of these institutions by the Puritans and their eighteenth-century heirs, the degree of attention given to the formation of conscience may nonetheless have increased, so much so that by the eighteenth century the relative balance of repression in the middle classes had changed. Women were now subject to more internal moral restraints than men. Hence, the conception that their sexuality was weaker may have had a basis in fact.

Along with a relative change in the balance of repression between men and women, there may also have been an absolute increase in the capacity of middle-class Englishmen and women to govern themselves, an increase which was both a result and a reinforcement of the demand for moral constancy. As discussed in chapter 2, the Puritans developed social forms within the family which were intended to, and apparently did, give their children, when grown, a great capacity to regulate their lives according to their own consciences. The forms of public life among Puritan adults often called for and made use of this capacity for moral self-direction.[1] This increase may well have nourished the conviction that thorough self-regulation of acts, deeds, words, and even desires and feelings was possible.

Whether the notion of superior feminine morality was a fiction or based on fact, the eighteenth-century hierarchy of gender came into being, I believe, to free men from the burden of the demand for moral constancy and the accompanying expectation that good persons will live the whole of their adult lives without significant moral failure—an expectation based on the belief that conscience can successfully govern the whole life of an adult.[2] There are many texts of eighteenth- and nineteenth-century English culture which illustrate this point, but none is more subtle than Samuel Richardson's *Pamela; or, Virtue Rewarded*, published in 1740.[3] The novel thoroughly embodied the new ideas of male and female, and did much to promote them both in England and on the Continent. Received with acclaim upon publication and frequently reprinted in the eighteenth century, *Pamela* established a new fictional genre in which a heroine exemplifying superior sexual and moral purity is subject to the threats and wiles of lustful men.[4]

The new idea of woman did not go unchallenged. Fielding vigorously upheld the belief that an alive and conscious sexuality did not deprive a woman—or a man—of moral goodness. But the success of the Richardsonian perspective can be measured by the extraordinary degree to which the "official" culture of late-eighteenth- and nineteenth-century England espoused the idea of the pure woman. The world of prostitution and pornography was the sexual underside of this public culture; in that world women were to be used, and abused, as purely sexual objects. Something similar, it turns out, already occurs in *Pamela.*

On the face of it, *Pamela* is an eminently moral tale. The title figure is a young servant of a noble lady (her own family having fallen on hard times). The death of her mistress leaves Pamela in the care of the noblewoman's son, the young, wealthy, rakish, and essentially good-hearted Mr. B., who takes a strong fancy to her. She repels his advances. Frightened by his anger and his intentions, Pamela attempts to return to the safety of her parents' home, but this never comes to pass. First, her master persuades her to delay her departure; then, after unsuccessfully and only halfheartedly attempting to rape her, he has her abducted to another of his estates, where he hopes in time she will assent to his wishes. Coming to love her, Mr. B. proposes to make her his mistress, a proposal she firmly rejects. Impressed by her virtue in the face of his power, he finally offers to marry her. She accepts this proposal with delight, since he strongly attracts her in spite of his attempts upon her innocence. Virtue is rewarded, as the subtitle of the book says; the servant girl marries her master.

Pamela's virtue is more powerful than Mr. B.'s challenge to it, although the cards are stacked heavily in his favor. His servants watch over her, the walls and gates of his estates imprison her, and she is no match for his physical strength. What is more, he is a master and she a servant; he is noble and wealthy, she insignificant and poor; he is a man, she a woman. How can she defend herself? Yet her virtue is strong enough to allow her to resist him—and finally to convert him. *Pamela* is a tale of virtue's potency.

There is much in the tale to make the reader respond to Pamela's distress. In his anger, Mr. B. finds it agreeable to humiliate her. He does so by making her feel little and helpless before his aggressive and hostile power. Her weakness pleases him. Not surprisingly, she fears her master's attacks, since they pose a real threat to her. They would be less threatening were she neither a woman nor a servant, but she is both. What little Pamela has can be taken away by her master.

He can deprive her of her chastity and her virtue (in the limited but important sense of her virginity before marriage). He nearly does so. He can (and does) take away the limited freedom of action she has as a female servant. He likewise takes away the small privacy her position permits her. He steals her letters and invades her room. He has the power to dismiss her from her job and to reduce her social position, low as it is. Finally, he can deprive her of her public reputation as a pure and honest girl.

But perhaps Pamela's greatest humiliation is that her master believes he has the *right*, by virtue of his social position, to do these things to her. Apart from his power to dismiss her, however, he has no true claim to this right. Her weakness, coupled with his power, enables him to behave tyranically without much fear of what others will do to him. Thus his sexual aggression and sadism have free rein. Why, then, would Pamela *not* fear Mr. B.'s sexuality, linked as it is to aggression and sadism? Why, moreover, would she not fear the sexuality of any man whose capacity to control and to harm her is so great? What resources can she draw upon if her refusal to answer her master's desire inspires hostility and violence? When she resists Mr. B., he attempts to rape her and does abduct her. He punishes her for resisting his desire by violating, or attempting to violate, her body, her space, and her privacy.

Here is the stuff of serious drama (and quite often melodrama). Early in the tale the young servant, expecting to return to her parents, prepares a new outfit, something appropriate to their simple way of life. It turns out to be quite charming. Pretending not to recognize Pamela in her new clothes, Mr. B. toys with her; "He came up to me," she tells her parents, "and took me by the Hand, and said, Whose pretty Maiden are you? —I dare say you are *Pamela*'s sister, you are so like her. So neat, so clean, so pretty! Why, Child, you far surpass your Sister *Pamela!*" Embracing and kissing her, he says, "[Y]ou are very pretty, Child; I would not be so

free with *Sister*, you may believe; but I must kiss *you*" (61).[5]
Mr. B. delights in the helplessness of his young servant, and
for all of his morality, Richardson is very much captured by
fantasies of women as objects of male domination, aggression, and sadism. I hesitate to call these masculine fantasies,
since women (for better or worse) can enjoy them too. *Pamela* was highly popular among novel-reading women in
Richardson's own time.

A chief element of Richardson's fantasy is that, despite
her fear, Pamela likes the aggressive and even the hostile elements of Mr. B.'s sexuality; they are, as she sees them, aspects of his vigor, his masculinity, his dangerous yet attractive power. Consider Pamela's encounters with a bull.
Imprisoned in one of Mr. B.'s country estates under the
guard of the crude and ugly Mrs. Jewkes, she finds a rare opportunity to escape when the back door to the garden, which
borders upon a pasture, is by chance unlocked. Lurking in
the pasture is a bull which Pamela knows has already attacked "the poor Cook-maid" (128). Pamela makes a first attempt to escape, retreats from the bull, timorously tries
once more, and again fails:

> I had got as far again, as I was before, out of the Back-
> door; and I looked, and saw the Bull, as I thought, be-
> tween me and the Door; and another Bull coming to-
> wards me the other way: Well, thought I, here is double
> Witchcraft, to be sure! Here is the Spirit of my Master
> in one Bull, and Mrs. *Jewkes*'s in the other; and now I
> am gone, to be sure! O help! cry'd I, like a Fool, and run
> back to the Door, as swift as if I flew. When I got the
> Door in my Hand, I ventur'd to look back, to see if
> these supposed Bulls were coming; and I saw they were
> only two poor Cows, a grazing in distant Places, that
> my Fears had made all this Rout about. (137)

Pamela's bulls—both real and imagined—are sexual and
potent. They are at once dangerous and attractive, unlike
the poor cows, who are neither. One of the imagined bulls
embodies the spirit of Mrs. Jewkes, who represents Mr. B's

sexuality because she promotes his sexual ends. She also represents Pamela's own sexuality, often proposing to Pamela that the girl is in fact sexually interested in Mr. B. The young servant girl, disgusted by the idea, firmly rejects it. Richardson makes it clear, however, that Mrs. Jewkes speaks the truth.

The days and hours leading up to Pamela's marriage and first night with Mr. B. reveal her attraction to his threatening sexuality. She happily anticipates but also fears the wedding ceremony, for it marks a change of condition. The outcome of her new dependency is most uncertain: like any young and virginal bride, she is giving herself up to a man who is "half strange" to her; whether he will use her well or ill, she observes, is "only to be proved by the Event" (286).[6] But she dreads the wedding day for another reason that she cannot so easily discover. "[W]hat ails me, I wonder! . . . which makes me often sigh involuntarily, and damps, at times, the Pleasures of my delightful Prospects!" (279). She is unaware of what the reader knows: that she fears the wedding night and her first experience of sex, with a man who is, and must be, in her eyes, half stranger.

What scares her about sex? A new and unfamiliar intimacy? The prospect of penetration? Neither. She fears that Mr. B., in his power, will force her to play a part in an elaboration of the impure, gross, and crude aspects of sexuality. Knowing this, Mr. B. attempts to reassure her; *he* has made no crude mention of the wedding night! "But now, my dearest *Pamela*, that you have seen a Purity on my Side, as nearly imitating your own, as our Sex can shew to yours; . . . why all this Concern, why all this affecting, yet sweet Confusion!" (281).

In fact, he is not true to the spirit of these words, for shortly before the wedding night he teases her. He is amused by his ability to force the gross and vulgar elements of sex upon her. To fill the short time while he is away, Mr. B. asks Mrs. Jewkes to tell his new wife a pleasant tale. The servant demurs, fearing that her bawdy stories would be unsuitable for Pamela, but he insists that she tell one anyway, while he is still there. This alarms Pamela:

Why, Sir, said [Mrs. Jewkes], I knew a bashful young
Lady, as Madam may be, marry'd to——— Dear Mrs.
Jewkes, interrupted I, no more of your Story, I beseech
you! I don't like the Beginning of it. Go on, Mrs.
Jewkes, said my Master. No, pray, Sir, don't require it,
said I; pray don't. Well, said he, then we'll have it another time, Mrs. *Jewkes.*" (293)

But Pamela is also pleased by Mr. B.'s capacity to domi-
nate her and to force her into sex, with its gross and crude
side; it thrills her without her being aware of it. As the evening of the first night draws near, the quiet and gentle day
which Mr. B. has arranged for Pamela is rudely interrupted
by three of Mr. B.'s male friends, who come impromptu, not
knowing of the wedding. She timidly looks at them out the
window: "three mad Rakes they seem'd to be, . . . setting up
a Hunting-note, as soon as they came to the Gate, that made
the Courtyard echo again, and smacking their Whips in
Concert" (291).

Mr. B.'s friends delight in the use of their whips, which
makes them masters, not only riders, of their mounts. Their
huntsmen's bravado makes them grand. Their horns reso-
nate throughout the courtyard. Straight on the heels of this
scene, Pamela anticipates the terrors of the nuptial bed: "So
I went up to my Chamber, and saw (what made my Heart
throb) Mrs. *Jewkes*'s officious Pains to put the Room in Order for a Guest, that however welcome, as now my Duty
teaches me to say, is yet dreadful to me to think of " (291).

Richardson creates an unconscious for Pamela—an aspect of her mind and feeling which the reader knows better
than she does—for we sense that she finds Mr. B.'s aggression attractive, even when she doesn't know this herself. In
her description early in the novel of Mr. B.'s attempt to rape
her, she shows this unacknowledged attraction. Hidden in
her closet, waiting for her to go to bed, Mr. B. moves a bit; although Pamela is frightened by the noises she hears, she pro-
ceeds to undress. "I pulled off my Stays, and my Stockens,
and my Gown, all to an Under-petticoat; and then hearing a

rustling again in the Closet, I said, God protect us! but before I say my Prayers, I must look into this Closet. And so was going to it slip shod, when, O dreadful! out rush'd my Master, in a rich silk and silver Morning Gown" (66). In his attempt upon her, Mr. B. does scare Pamela dreadfully. Of this she is aware. But what she does not acknowledge is that he attracts her as well. The reader is aware of her desire through her own description of Mr. B.'s expensive dress.[7]

Why does Mr. B. attract Pamela, even as he seeks to rape her? As the quoted passage shows, his wealth appeals to her; the power of money is sexy to Pamela, who has none. However, there is more to Mr. B.'s sexiness than his money or social position, both of which Pamela will share once she is married to him. As the bulls and the horsemen make clear, Richardson imagines that Pamela wants to be forced into the sex which her own purity and modesty would have her avoid. It is this idea, well known to the modern male and female imagination, which allows Richardson to treat Pamela's powerlessness before Mr. B.'s attacks not just as serious drama, but as comedy and farce. In his attempts to violate her purity, which from the point of view of her conscience are truly threatening, Mr. B. seeks something which Pamela unconsciously also desires, however much she resists it: the defeat of that conscience and its demands.

Pamela very much wants to be, and is to a large degree, a good girl. The intensity of this desire is shown in her constant moral self-examination, her charity toward others, and her concern that others be good. But this desire to be good poses real problems for her sexuality. Modesty, refinement, and purity constitute essential elements of her concept of moral goodness. They oppose a free and ample sexuality which must include much that is not refined, purified, or transformed into something more elevated. Pamela's sexual interests are thus under severe attack by her own conscience, captured as it is by the notion of purity.

She wants to be good, as her parents want her to be. In fact, she tells her tale through letters to her parents, who are for her the paradigms of moral goodness. She attempts to orient herself exclusively to their demands and perspective. When they write to her, they make it clear that they want her to be as pure as she herself thinks she should be. She looks to them for security, too. When Mr. B. threatens her, she writes them, "I long to come to you," to return to the parental nest (51). When Parson Arthur Williams, a good-hearted clergyman hoping to free her from Mr. B.'s clutches, proposes marriage to her, she writes to her father and mother, "I have no Mind to marry. I had rather live with you" (130). In her letters, then, Pamela addresses herself to the human counterparts of her own conscience, who, like her conscience, offer her a secure, steady, and familiar source of comfort. The parent who plays a distinct role in the story is Pamela's father; her mother remains a shadowy figure and never appears. It is the father who comes to reclaim his daughter from her peril and who discovers that she has remained innocent after all. Her power to remain a virgin in the face of Mr. B.'s threats rests largely upon her desire to be a good girl for her father, but that desire makes an easy sexuality difficult even after marriage, for how can she be her father's good girl and still be sexual? Submission to Mr. B.'s power and authority through marriage means a sharp and remarkable rise in her own status and power— from a servant girl to a lady of quality. (To conform to her idea of her own goodness, however, she must describe her increase in power as a greater capacity to help others.)[8] Yielding to Mr. B. also brings her into the world of adult sexuality. He has the power (as brutal master) to force her and the authority (as husband) to require her to submit to his sexual wishes. In her subjection she gains the freedom to violate her own purity. When Mr. B. acts forcefully against her desire to remain pure, he attacks an aspect of her conscience, the loss of which is psychically quite costly to her. Since she herself does not have the power to attack her conscience directly, she is drawn to Mr. B., who has the will to attack and the power to defeat the father within her.

Mr. B.'s power, in all its aspects, makes him more sexually and emotionally attractive to Pamela than his competitor for her hand, Williams. The parson is a poor man. Apart from what he earns by teaching Latin to village children, he is wholly dependent upon Mr. B. for whatever income or future he has—"all his Dependence is upon my Master," Pamela writes; he even owes Mr. B. money (106). Socially speaking, he is little compared to Mr. B. and will never be much. At best, he can be an unimportant village curate who must always rely on the good will of Pamela's master. Williams does not come off well in physical strength or courage either; he cuts a pathetic figure when he is attacked by robbers at the dam on his return from a visit to Pamela. He describes the attack thus: "They romag'd my Pockets, . . . bruised my Head, and Face, and . . . typt me into the Dam, Crying, Lie there, Parson, till to-morrow! My shins and Knees were bruis'd much in the Fall against one of the Stumps, and I had like to have been suffocated in Water and Mud. To be sure, I shan't be able to stir out this Day or two" (134–35).

Lacking force, he is no match for robbers, as he is no match for Mr. B. He even compares unfavorably to the bull. Pamela, the parson, and Mrs. Jewkes walk out to the pasture one day to look at the "ugly, grim, surly Creature, that hurt the poor Cook-maid" (133). Innocent of worldly affairs, Mr. Williams puts Pamela in great danger through his inability to keep secret her plan to escape. In the presence of Mrs. Jewkes, he indiscreetly points to the sunflower on the edge of the garden, near which Pamela hides the letters to her parents which he then picks up and sends. "I was forc'd to be very reserved to him," Pamela says, "the poor Gentlemen has no Guard, no Caution at all" (133).

Moreover, he lacks the virility and aggressive sexuality of her master. He first reveals his love to her by looks of great "Solemnness" (129). "He is a sensible, sober young Gentleman" who "pays me great Respect," Pamela tells her parents, to whom he has written asking her hand in marriage, but "pray don't encourage him . . . tho', to be sure, he is a very good Man, and I am much oblig'd to him" (134). Pamela never tells them why she doesn't want him; if he is so good, civil, pious, and sober, why shouldn't she have him? He would seem perfectly suited to her own conscience and purity. But he cannot raise desire in Pamela by goodness alone. When her heart rather than her conscience speaks, the reader knows she would rather have Mr. B., who is less good but much more powerful.

Pamela never acknowledges that she is drawn to Mr. B.'s capacity to make her violate her own scruples; she never says to herself or to anyone else that she finds the bull, the horsemen, and the aggressive Mr. B. sexually attractive. She is young; the reader may wish that she would develop more honesty and self-knowledge as her story unfolds, but she is as innocent of her sexuality at the conclusion of her tale as when she began. She remains a little prude. She therefore makes her husband wholly responsible for her sexual intercourse with him. She has to do it; it is her duty as a wife. In this way she can be a good girl while being sexual; she can retain her claim to full purity as if she had never left her father. Even Mr. B. joins this charade, for he never says to her (even in marriage) that she herself wants him sexually, as he wants her. Neither he nor Pamela ever acknowledges that his aggression against her own purity is good inasmuch as it takes the side of her sexual interests against the tyranny of her own conscience. *Pamela* is not a tale of a girl's awakening to and acceptance of her own sexuality.

We never get Pamela's description of her first night in bed, for how could she relate to her parents what actually happened? We know that Mr. B. was no beast; in the first letter after her wedding night—written the next evening, for to write the morning after would have been indelicate —she tells her parents that she is fortunate in the man who has chosen her: "his Words are so pure, his ideas so chaste, and his whole Behaviour so sweetly decent, that never, surely, was so happy a Creature as your *Pamela!*" (295).

As I have said, Richardson uses for comic purposes Pamela's unwillingness to acknowledge either her sexual needs or her master's power to fulfill them. When he focuses on

Mr. B.'s humiliation of his young servant or takes the part of Pamela's desire for purity, the novel is a serious drama. But insofar as Pamela is forced to undergo what she really wants while vigorously asserting that she does not want it, the reader laughs. To create this laughter, the author need only show Pamela as innocent of her own desires; there is no need to have Mr. B. and others (in the end, all others) go along with her self-deception.

So why does Richardson have all of them agree? The answer lies in the eighteenth-century English ambivalence about purity and sexuality. Richardson's novel is built on two incompatible perceptions of what is occurring. One idea is purely moral, the other amoral and erotic. The moral idea is very clear: Pamela, having retained her purity under attack by a man of great power, is rewarded by his reform and his hand in marriage. This idea forms the moral surface of the tale, which Richardson takes care never to disturb. Pamela's wish to have her own purity violated works on a different level. No event overtly demonstrates her desire; no character worthy of respect acknowledges that she has it. Mrs. Jewkes makes it clear she thinks Pamela wants her way with Mr. B., but the older servant is an object of disgust. How crude of her, how "little Purity of Heart" (285) to suggest that Pamela wants the sexual experience Mr. B. offers her! Yet this is just the desire Richardson has given Pamela. Why does he not openly acknowledge the sexual feelings of his heroine?[9]

Richardson believes in the demands of purity in all their fullness, as Pamela does: "Her Maiden and Bridal Purity, which extended as well to her Thoughts as to her Words and Actions," he writes in his concluding remarks, "make her Character worthy of the Imitation of her Sex," whether of low or high station. He will have succeeded in his purpose as the "Editor" of her letters, he says, if the excellency of her mind and spirit inspires the minds of his worthy readers to emulate her; if they follow her example, they "intitle themselves to the Rewards, the Praises, and the Blessings, by which she was so deservedly distinguished" (412). The devotion to purity which Richardson gives to Pamela expresses the power of the same devotion within the author himself. Richardson is also an erotic being, one who knows the coercion purity and modesty can exercise over sexuality. "Pray try to subdue this Over-scrupulousness and unseasonable Timidity," says Mr. B. to his bride-to-be (281). In *Pamela*, Richardson expresses the eighteenth-century ambivalence about purity; he is captured by purity yet is acutely aware of what it costs him sexually. His fantasies of Pamela's desire for Mr. B. as rapist or sexual aggressor are masculine in a sense not at first obvious: they are pleasurable fantasies of his own rape, of someone forcing *him* into the sexuality which his own conscience rejects.

For all of his insight into the tyranny that purity can exercise over sexuality, Richardson does not give up his high valuation of Pamela's purity. He therefore neither recognizes nor allows any respectable character to recognize that Mr. B.'s attempts to violate Pamela's modesty and refinement answer her own desires, and in fact serve her well. If he were to acknowledge the constructive function of Mr. B.'s aggression, he would have to acknowledge, as a point of morality, that sexual purity has its limits and that Pamela's conscience asks too much of her. Richardson is unwilling, however, to launch a moral critique of his own devotion to purity. He therefore becomes dishonest and sentimental, for he uses the sincerely meant morality of his novel to disguise his amoral and erotic themes.

Richardson also gives Pamela an unblemished claim to sexual purity as a means of defense against the aggression and sadism of Mr. B. Whatever he does to her, she believes herself to be a better person. He has the legal, social, and economic power, but she has the virtue—a conviction he and the other characters in the novel all come to share.

The claim to purity, which ultimately plays a part in Mr. B.'s reform, also furnishes an enticing opportunity for his cruelty. He does not always seek to overcome Pamela's purity simply to answer his sexual needs; sometimes he tries to defeat her chastity and modesty purely in anger, in order to harm. When he learns of her plans to escape from her imprisonment with the aid of Parson Williams, Mr. B. tells Mrs. Jewkes that, while he would do nothing to her himself, he could bear, out of revenge and slighted love, to see Pamela raped; then she would fill the "Woods and Groves" with lamentations for the loss of her innocence, "which the romantick Idiot makes such a work about" (144–45). Who will be the instrument of this final humiliation? Pamela fears it will be the servant Mr. B. has sent to guard her, his trusty Swiss, Monsieur Colbrand, whom she describes as "a Giant of a Man, . . . large bon'd, and scraggly, and a Hand!—I never saw such an one in my Life. He has great staring Eyes, like the Bull's that frighten'd me so" (147–48).

Pamela's purity thus functions in opposing ways in Richardson's novel. It is to be heeded, yet it is to be overcome by the sexual aggression of Mr. B.; it is a major source of Pamela's self-esteem and a defense against Mr. B.'s hostility and sadism, yet it is a claim which cannot stand the light of day—a sentimental falsehood. The meanings of Pamela's purity for Mr. B. are also contradictory: her purity is morally admirable and charmingly maidenly, yet "over-nice" (294); his attack upon her purity serves her best interests, yet it also answers his desire to harm her.

Richardson allows a clear recognition of the hostile intent of Mr. B.'s aggression in what I have called the moral surface of the tale, but he leaves its constructive purpose and function to the subtext. The author's dramatic elaboration of the positive meanings of Mr. B.'s aggression against Pamela's conscience is a major achievement,[10] but Richardson is unwilling to attack openly the irrational tendencies of purity which create his heroine's problem. He wants to have his cake and eat it too: he wants her to have the pleasures of sex, impure as they may be, without having to give up the moral pleasures of purity. This cannot be, save in fantasy, yet it is the superb literary development of just this fantasy which makes the book so good.

I shall use the term *reciprocal hierarchy* to name the relation between Mr. B. and Pamela, for in the English social form of the eighteenth and nineteenth centuries, masculinity is superior to femininity and vice versa. Man is willing to overcome a woman's scruples, and therefore he is both better and worse than the woman he seeks. His virility makes him better (the woman lacks his animal force and will to power) and worse (his conscience is weak). A woman naturally listens to the moral voice within. Her femininity makes her better (she is ethically purer) and worse (her purity depends upon a lack of animal force and will to command). This view of men and women created a new set of complementary potencies. The purity of women made them dependent upon men, for men, unlike women, could be commanding and animal without violating their place in the hierarchy. Inasmuch as women needed animality and a forceful, dominating power in their own lives, they had to get it exclusively from men. And men, in their animality and amoral will to power, needed the civilizing presence of women.[11]

What makes woman morally pure is not her thorough observance of and submission to requirements of an external morality coming from a divine source. She is pure because of the power of her own moral conscience within her mind and heart; that conscience is so predominant that it blocks even the recognition of her own sexual needs. It is so strong that, save for the most exceptionally trying circumstances, her own moral voice is her master. The medieval expectation that all, even the best, will repeatedly sin no longer exists.

The new idea of goodness applied to all. To limit its cost to men, a new division of labor was also created, and women were given the full burden of carrying out the demands of a life completely governed by conscience. Men were still to be virtuous (for which they needed the help of women), but they could be less than completely virtuous and still be true men. The exemplary value of masculinity was found not in moral perfection but in the will to command. The demands of conscience were laid to a certain extent upon women.

The peculiar reciprocity of this division of moral labor, in which men are better than women and women better than men, expresses a fundamentally contradictory attitude toward the worth of a life thoroughly lived under the rule of conscience. This ambivalent valuation has no necessary relation to gender and can be stated without any mention of male or female: a being in whom animal exuberance and a vigorous will to power are strong is both superior and inferior to one in whom conscience takes full control.

It is difficult for cultures and civilizations, as it is for individuals, to acknowledge in a thorough and constant way the contradictory valuations that constitute their very being. Prophets and intellectuals may point them out, but the forms of social life generally do not openly acknowledge them. Reciprocal hierarchies make the contradictions they express less apparent and less pressing by embodying the opposed values in different social categories. Contradictory beliefs about the relative worth of animality and moral purity would be most evident if all persons were expected to be both pure and lusty. Eighteenth-century English culture, like medieval culture to an extent, avoids this by calling upon men to exemplify animality and women moral purity. In this way the inconsistency of valuing moral purity both more and less than the will to power and animal vigor is made less obvious. The reciprocal hierarchy of gender, then, answers two different interests. As a division of labor, it fulfills the male desire to be free of the burdens of life thoroughly governed by conscience, for these can be left to the woman. As a symbolic form which both expresses and disguises a cultural contradiction, the reciprocal hierarchy answers an interest not peculiarly male or female, since contradictory attitudes about being good and the wish to have the conflict buried are not the exclusive province of either sex.

Similar as the medieval opposition of prince to monk was to the hierarchy of gender, it could not adequately answer eighteenth-century English psychological needs. The eighteenth-century English church had no monastic orders; furthermore, the earlier reciprocal hierarchy was symbolically inadequate to the new needs of the 1700s. The medieval opposition was spiritual. It contrasted the man who lived his life in prayer and worship, straining every fiber of his being to come closer to God, with the man who, enjoying the world and its pleasures, was farther from God. The purity which Pamela embodies is moral. The eighteenth-century heroine does not represent the struggle to know God and to be in his bosom; her goodness, even her goodness in relation to God, is fully expressed in her moral success. The monk, the world-renouncer, was therefore an inappropriate symbol for the Enlightenment belief that moral purity is possible for individuals who remain very much in this world.

The hierarchy of gender not only freed men from having to live a thoroughly moral life, but it sustained them in their role as the more powerful of the two sexes. The traditional Western belief in the superior worth of men had supported (and been supported by) the greater legal, social, and political power of males. Enlightenment ideas of women provided new arguments for their age-old exclusion from public life, as well as arguments for their new exclusion from commerce. The Puritans had expected that women would take part in commerce inasmuch as they were to share in the management of the household economy, which produced as well as consumed. But in the Enlightenment idea of gender, women were too innocent and elevated to take part in the dirty rough and tumble of either politics or business.

Women nonetheless gained a kind of power through Enlightenment ideas of gender—moral power. As exemplars of moral perfection from the late seventeenth century on, they played a major role in social movements devoted to the reform of manners and morals: in matters of sex (including prostitution and pornography), temperance, gambling, piety, the family, marriage, courtship, and child-rearing.[12] As exemplars of moral purity, women, like the medieval monk, were subject to the suspicion that they did not in actuality possess the virtue they were supposed to embody. How could these contradictory feelings about women not arise? After all, to make them naturally pure did not relieve them from the reality of being human, and therefore sexual. Even Richardson himself communicates this double sense of a woman's nature in his portrayal of Pamela. It was not only a sense of reality which led eighteenth-century culture to attribute sexual desire to pure females, an attribution which Mary Poovey aptly calls one of the paradoxes of eighteenth-century propriety.[13] The complementary potencies assigned to men and women no doubt also had a part in creating this double perspective. If women needed and were attracted to male animality, lacking it themselves, did this not suggest to eighteenth-century culture that there was an animality in women which created their positive response to men? Perhaps it was naturally weaker, but it was—and had to be—still there.

One of the most popular and influential modern theories of purity is offered by Mary Douglas in *Purity and Danger: An Analysis of the Concepts of Pollution and Taboo.* Her theory appears doubtful in the light of the argument and evidence just presented. Douglas begins with an analysis of the idea of dirt, arguing that dirt is something out of place. "Uncleanness or dirt is that which must be excluded if a pattern or order is to be maintained."[14] She continues by pointing out that one way of dealing with the challenge of things which do not fit into a conceptual scheme is to avoid or condemn those things. "Ideas about separating, purifying, demarcating and punishing transgressions have as their main function to impose system on an inherently untidy experience."[15] Order is maintained only by exaggerating difference. This is how Douglas says the idea of purity is created: something is made pure to defend it from things which do not fit.

My analysis of *Pamela* poses a challenge to Douglas' theory. The conflict between the sexual, aggressive, or animal side of Mr. B. on the one hand, and his own (and Pamela's) conscientious attitudes on the other, is an encounter between two equally coherent but inconsistent hierarchies of value. Given these opposed perspectives, the pure is just as much out of place as far as male culture is concerned, as male animality is out of place from the point of view of female culture. Yet female purity is not seen as dirty from the perspective of male sexuality. Its moral perfection relieves men of a burden they would rather not carry. It is created in order to maintain room for male expression in the realm of sexuality. Female purity is not supposed to fit the values of male animality and is created precisely because it goes so far beyond them. We cannot, as Douglas proposes, take Lord Chesterfield's remark that dirt is matter out of place as an adequate guide to an understanding of purity and pollution. The remark suggests that what is impure has no power to create order on its own behalf,[16] but this is just what male sexuality does in Richardson's novel.

In eighteenth- and nineteenth-century English culture, the sexual and hierarchical ordering of the social world was challenged by the egalitarian conviction that the fundamental element of society is the person. Hierarchy is only a secondary aspect of social organization. When people meet as persons, they meet as equals, whatever their sex. They differ in what they make of their personhood; there can be a ranking of people in respect to the use, abuse, and neglect of personhood, but what makes someone a person can be found in equal degree in all.

When we encounter one another in egalitarian society, therefore, we do not fundamentally meet each other as men or women, old or young, ignorant or learned, high- or lowborn. These are all externals, morally and socially relevant in some ways but not basic to our mutual relations. As persons, we meet one another not in our difference but in our sameness. This attitude toward others calls for an end to the recognition of difference and hierarchy as fundamental social facets; inasmuch as we meet as persons, we meet as beings of equal worth. The idea that the fundamental social unit is the person has made a particularly great difference in Western law. Nonetheless, Enlightenment notions of masculine and feminine have shown considerable power well into the twentieth century. What accounts for the health of these hierarchical conceptions, despite their inconsistency with the egalitarian tendencies of modern Western culture?

To some extent, their survival is a testimony to the power of men to enforce a division of labor which both justifies their power and frees them from the burdens of moral purity. The hierarchy has also been supported by women because of the superior moral status and power it gives them. Behind these narrow interests lies the continuing power of the idea of possible moral purity in this world—and the now widespread capacity for individual moral self-regulation promoted by the Puritans. The Puritans developed techniques to increase the capacity for moral self-regulation and rejected the relief given by the medieval cycle of sin, guilt, and repentance, where failure was expected and therefore given a sort of cultural sanction. In new conceptions of male and female, a source of relief was developed that reduced the discomfort created by the all-powerful conscience—a pain not so much acute as unremitting. But this relief was only for men.

Conclusion

$\mathbf{M}$ichel Foucault writes that from the confession of medieval penance to the many forms of self-disclosure available today, "the confession was, and still remains, the general standard" for the West, "governing the production of true discourse on sex."[1] Pamela's letters to her parents are certainly an example of a confessional discourse whose covert if not overt subject is her own sexuality. What is most remarkable is that her sexual orientation to the world is as steady as her morality. Richardson has her respond with a sexual tone to many of the men in her world, with delight in Mr. B.'s gorgeous clothes, with a sexualized fear of his monstrous Swiss servant, and with disappointment in the pallid parson. Her creator has her respond with strong negative sexualized feelings to one of the women in her world, the disgusting Mrs. Jewkes, and with sexual narcissism to herself—her own clothes and appearance—and to circumstances where no one else is physically present, as in her encounter with cows which she takes for bulls. The author encourages the reader to feel that because Pamela's sexuality is steadily active, it is at the very core of her being.

Pamela's sexuality is steady also with respect to what attracts it. However much Mr. B. threatens her purity, he is from the very beginning of the tale the object of her desire.

Her sexual interest never shifts to anyone else. Before her marriage to Mr. B., her sexuality already possesses the steadiness which the Puritans required of husbands and wives.

In an older view of sexuality, well developed by classical Greek and Roman authors, Pamela would not have been as constantly and actively sexual in her orientation. As many of the classical authors see it, sexual desire and interest naturally fluctuates in both men and women. Sexual feelings may rise to great intensity, then fall into quiescence. The power of sexual interest lies not in its steadiness but in its capacity to be overwhelmingly but temporarily intense. This belief in the oscillating and transitory character of sexuality persisted through the medieval period. It was a commonplace truth for Montaigne. The ardor of male love of women, he writes, "is active, scorching, and intense," but it is an "impetuous and fickle flame, subject to fits and lulls." In intercourse with women, the impulse is violent, but there is no steadiness to a man's desire.[2] The same is true for women's sexual interest. Today, the term *lust* continues to embody the older sense of the passionate and temporary nature of sexual interest.

Indeed, *lust* is a good description of Mr. B.'s sexual feeling toward Pamela. His unsatisfied desire so aggravates him that at one moment he is willing even to attempt rape, but the intensity of his desire is also a sign of its unsteadiness, as Pamela well understands. Once he has her, will he continue to want her? In the older view of sexuality, the answer must be no. Enjoyment destroys our interest in sex. As Montaigne says, in sexual love there is nothing but "a frantic desire for what flees from us."[3] Richardson gives Mr. B. a kind of sexuality already highly elaborated in late-seventeenth-century English comedy. Once Mr. B. has what he wants from Pamela, there is no reason to suppose he will continue to take the same pleasure in her year in and year out. In fact he does not, for in Richardson's sequel to *Pamela*, which describes Pamela's marriage to Mr. B., the husband's attentions soon wander.[4]

In light of the traditional view of sexuality as a temporary orientation, the constancy of Pamela's sexual feelings is notable. In fulfilling the Puritan demand upon conjugal love even before she is married, she exemplifies a notion of the possible steadiness of sexuality already developed by the Puritans. She is interested only in Mr. B. and remains interested in him, but her sexual interest is also constant in a way not envisaged by the Puritans. It more or less colors all her experience, as she describes it. This, no doubt, is the reason for the persistently pornographic tone of Richardson's "moral" novel, and the steadiness of her sexual orientation is not something the Puritans would ever have desired. Why did Richardson give her such a sexual self?

Weber's analysis of the Puritan ambitions for the human psyche provides the basis for an answer. He writes that the Puritans attempted to make men and women into ethical personalities, people who acted on constant moral motives throughout their lives. Conscience had to represent the very center of their being. To the extent that new techniques of self-regulation gave conscience a new and steady power over men and women within the Puritan tradition (as may have occurred through a child-raising program like Locke's), conscience no doubt seemed to represent their core self.

The new power of conscience to represent the core of personality posed a serious problem for the "old" fluctuating sexuality in its competition with conscience. Because of the constancy of its regulative power, conscience gained a higher value than before. It could claim to represent what it could not easily have claimed to represent before: ourselves. But what could be said on behalf of the older sexuality? However much it could be expected to overpower us in its moments of intensity, it could not claim to represent the steady core of the self. If the self was to be defined by its constant motives, then sexuality could be only marginal to the core of the self; it could not claim to have the same standing that the constant conscience had. The old animality was no match for the new conscience.

Sexuality, to defend itself, took on the character of its opponent. It, too, claimed to be a constant and potent motive which colored all of life; in so doing, it could claim to represent the core of the self. The battle for the value of sexuality must be fought on the terrain of Pamela's psyche, and not Mr. B.'s, because Pamela has the constant conscience. The fluctuating power of Mr. B.'s morality gives his conscience no claim to represent who he really is. Pamela must embody the new sexuality because she has the new conscience. Ultimately, however, the sexuality Richardson gives to his pure Pamela became standard for both males and females in much of the Western world, for men were expected more and more to exert the steady moral self-control which eighteenth-century England particularly had imposed upon women.

Although modern men and women regard confession as the way to make their steady sexuality speak and reveal its truth, it should not be supposed, Foucault writes, that the one who confesses already knows the secrets that sex harbors.[5] Far from it. Sex is something so hidden and elusive that we can only hope to discover its aims and methods through the most extraordinary labors of record keeping, collection, and analysis. Pamela's letters provide the material for analysis, but Pamela herself remains unaware of the full meaning of what she says and does.

Why must sex be so mysterious to modernity? Montaigne did not find it so obscure. Our analysis provides an answer. Inasmuch as sexuality is at the core of our personality, it must be constant in its activity. This is so by the very definition of what constitutes a self for the Puritan tradition. Yet sexuality persists, it seems, in having the fluctuating and transitory character acknowledged by the older view. In one's experience, sexual interest and orientation toward others is not always steady. This fluctuation poses no problem of interpretation for the older point of view. From the modern point of view, however, sexuality can only appear to be absent, since it must always (really) be at work. Modern men and women thus suppose that sex is hidden (rather than absent) when it is not present. This makes sex fundamentally mysterious.

In the first volume of his *History of Sexuality,* Foucault rejects the belief that from the seventeenth century onward the fundamental fact about sex in the West has been the attempt by morality to prohibit it, deny its existence, and condemn it to silence.[6] To some extent, my analysis of the relations between conscience and sexuality sustains Foucault's claim. For the unconsciousness of one's own sexuality is clearly more than the outcome of an unwillingness to acknowledge sexual things about oneself of which the conscience heartily disapproves. The mystery of sex is in large part a function of affirming it to be unceasingly active. Far from being a denial, the mystery is a full-scale affirmation of sex's presence even when it appears to be absent. Yet Foucault is wrong to suppose that sexuality's mystery is not a response to the power of conscience. It may not be as much an outcome of the censoring powers of conscience as Freud may sometimes think, but the mystery is an indirect outcome of conscience's new power to command and to control. It is because of the new conscience that a new sense of sex's mysterious place in the human psyche comes about. Far from simply repressing sex, conscience also creates it.

Foucault's failure to see the causal link between the new conscience and the new sexuality allows him to place the origins of the modern mysteriousness of sex in the medieval practice of confession. There he finds that sex was already something "hidden," only to be discovered by the most careful inquiries of the confessor.[7] However, the evidence goes firmly against Foucault. In light of the careful and systematic survey of manuals of confession and other texts bearing upon the practice of confession which Thomas N. Tentler has published in *Sin and Confession on the Eve of the Reformation,* one would have to say that sexuality as such was not regarded as harboring a great secret. Sexual sins, like other sins, had to be discovered by the confessor to achieve the absolution and edification of the penitent; this sometimes required detailed and delicate questions. Clavasio's *Summa* (1500, commonly called the *Angelica*) says that questions must be asked, for "the good confessor must try to discover the sins of confused, forgetful, and difficult penitents." The questions were required not because sexuality was by its very nature obscure, but because of "human simplicity and shame"—very different matters.[8] There is nothing peculiarly obscure about sexuality, and the *Angelica* suggests that every sin may have special circumstances that require special investigation.

The most complete program of interrogation in the late medieval literature on confession is the treatise *On the Confession of Masturbation*, attributed to Jean Gerson.[9] Here, too, the author makes it clear that the problem for the confessor lies in the shame and unwillingness of penitents to talk about their deeds and desires. There is nothing mysterious about what they are hiding. He advises the confessor to begin by inquiring, " '[F]riend, do you remember when you were young, about ten or twelve years old, your rod *(virga)* or virile member *(membrum pudendi)* ever stood erect?' " If the penitent answers no, the author says he must be lying, since this happens to all boys unless they are abnormal. If the penitent still refuses to tell the truth, the author advises this question: " 'Friend, didn't you touch or rub your member (virgam) the way boys usually do?' If he entirely denies that he ever held it or rubbed it in that state it is not possible to proceed further except in expressing amazement and saying that it is not credible: exhorting him to remember his salvation; that he is before God; that it is most serious to lie in confession, and the like."[10]

Tentler says that the aggressive tone and clinical detail of this manual are not characteristic of the guides to the practice of confession.[11] Even if this text were typical, it would offer no support for the thesis that the medieval confessional treated sex as essentially mysterious. Quite the opposite; sex is treated as a common and understandable phenomenon. The same cannot be said for the sexuality which modernity imagines as the opponent of the constant conscience.

There is a common notion that the history of civilizations is in the long run the history of the internalization of moral norms. This notion must be qualified. Looking at matters in terms of millennia, internal sanctions have certainly come to play a greater and greater role in governing men's and women's behavior while external punishments have come to play a somewhat weaker role. But internalization is not a sophisticated enough concept to explain the actual movement of moral practices in the history of culture.

In a broad sense we do know what internalization means. Moral requirements which were once experienced by individuals as coming from outside themselves and which have been enforced by threats of punishment and promises of reward come to be experienced as expressions of themselves. The need to conform to the moral demand then comes from within. But, as should be evident, a moral demand is not swallowed and digested like a piece of food, nor is it suddenly experienced as an aspect of one's own self. Moral demands are related in complex ways to social practices and expectations, forms of education, and means of punishment in the case of failure. It is not enough to look at whether moral ideas are internalized; we must also see how these ideas are treated when experienced as coming from within.

A common idea is that in the medieval culture of sin, guilt, and repentance, the expectation of failure was built upon the fact that people were not wholeheartedly committed to the values of the church. This may not have been the case. Perhaps the cycle was built on a different idea; namely, that even when people do experience moral demands as coming from within themselves, they do not normally have the ability or power to maintain them in full force—to organize intentions or to compel their own conduct and feelings around these demands at all times and in all places.

The cycle of sin, guilt and repentance can better be seen as resulting from the unavailability of techniques and methods for learning how to control oneself. When we come to the ethic of constancy, we are seeing not so much an intensification of the commitment to moral norms as a development of a belief that people can successfully control their behavior and feelings in a much more thorough way than was previously believed. There is no evidence to indicate that, in the culture of constancy, people experienced moral demands as coming from within themselves more strongly than in the culture of sin, guilt, and repentance. The difference does not depend on the degree of internalization, but on the expectations, psychological techniques, and social supports for the idea that one can avoid failure in meeting the daily moral demands of life.

In this respect, Freud's assessment of the history of civilization must also be revised. The idea of internalization is too simplistic and is insufficiently sociological. The Puritans and those who followed them developed techniques for controlling their behavior and feelings. They also developed social forms to sustain this high degree of moral compliance. These things must be looked at not simply as matters of individual psychology but as social inventions and cultural forms.

In *The Protestant Temperament*, Philip Greven isolates three distinctive religious temperaments in seventeenth-, eighteenth-, and nineteenth-century America. He calls these temperaments evangelical, moderate, and genteel. The evangelicals "were dominated by a persistent and virtually inescapable hostility to the self and all of its manifestations." They aimed at becoming people who were so self-denying, unwillful, and submissive that their whole character and life would be filled up with the will of God and would be controlled by Him. Evangelicals "always felt most at peace when least free to act, to think, to feel, or to will for themselves."[12]

Greven's second category, the moderates, were people who sought a middle way, necessitating a wide range of compromises. They believed in self-denial, but not to the extent of annihilating the self. They had to accommodate both ascetic tendencies and life-affirming or self-affirming tendencies. They kept themselves within fairly narrow bounds of feeling and behavior. "Their central concern was always self-control."[13] The third category, the genteel, were people who basically liked themselves and who felt a sense of self-confidence that set them apart from both the evangelicals and the moderates.

Greven's argument is that all three temperaments existed throughout the whole of American Protestant religious history, and by implication he suggests that it is wrong to see any development in which one or another form of temperament rises to a dominant position in the culture. If he were correct, and if his views were extended to the English case (as might well be attempted), there would be an argument against one of the theses of this book, for I have argued that the Puritan attempt at integration of sensuality and conscience was replaced as a dominant cultural form by a concern for purity and by more severe antagonism between the claims of sensuality and the claims of conscience and morality. Richardson's *Pamela* expresses these tensions.

Greven wants to break down culture to a set of individual temperaments or milieus and to argue that there is no single attitude which prevails throughout most of the culture. There is no reason to agree with this premise. After all, it may well be that there were many Puritans between 1620 and 1660 who were what Greven calls evangelical in temperament. Nonetheless, the writings about marriage in this period are basically moderate or, as I have called them, integrative. I would also argue that the popularity and cultural potency of *Pamela* and all that followed in its vein illustrate a shift in general cultural dominance, in which integrative ideas with respect to marriage and sexuality are replaced by ideas with a more oppositional character (purity versus sexuality), and that these ideas come to play an increasingly important role in the moral culture of eighteenth-century England.

Why did the idea of purity come to serve men's interests so strongly in the eighteenth and nineteenth centuries? The answer I have suggested is that men were concerned about their own moral purity and discovered a way to transfer some of this burden onto women. I also wish to emphasize, however, that as a symbolic form the idea of female purity answered the interests of the culture in general, since the ambivalence about the worth of leading a fully moral life was shared by women as well as men.

It would be foolish to ignore the extreme degree to which seventeenth- and eighteenth-century English culture was formed by men. Men, by and large, wrote the sermons, treatises, discourses, and novels, the laws and the books about the laws; they, by and large, ran the public institutions of the country and claimed the right to run their families as well. There were women authors, but they wrote in a world of words mostly written by men. It is easy to conclude from this record of overwhelming masculine cultural power that the idea of female purity answered only masculine interests. Poovey says that the idea of the proper lady was the creation of bourgeois society, a society made by men for men.

But this view, which seems to express a solidarity with women, does not credit them with the moral burdens they actually bore within the Puritan tradition and the eighteenth-century culture that grew out of it. Whether the demand for moral and emotional constancy was put in starkly religious terms, as in Puritan sermons, or in the more purely moral terms of Richard Steele, it was a demand which, as its proponents saw it, no grown-up could properly evade. How, then, can we suppose that only men would feel ambivalent about it, that only men would need a way to deal with the conflicts created by the claims of constancy? Would a morally serious woman of the contemporary West likely be exempt from conflicting feelings about the emotional costs of this demanding ethic? If not, why should we suppose that things were any different for the many female readers of *Pamela?* The importance of a female reading public for the eighteenth-century novel is well known; contemporary observers such as Addison and Steele comment on it. The great popularity of Richardson's novels among female readers of his own time is also recognized. Why, then, should one not be willing to believe that Richardson's complex ways of dealing with purity and its costs appealed to women as well as men for the same fundamental reasons?

In light of this reasoning, several modern accounts of the

rise of female purity in the eighteenth century need modification. Keith Thomas writes that "the total desexualization of women" was the fullest expression of the male view that "women's function was a purely sexual one. . . . The virtue of women was relative to their function, and their function was to cater to the needs of men. For this task the first qualification was chastity," for chastity meant that a woman's sexual services were to be reserved for her husband alone. Her chastity was a kind of property whose ownership was vested first in her parents, who expected her to remain a virgin until her marriage. "Once married, her chastity was transferred to another owner." Her husband could then make use of her sexual services for his own pleasure. According to Thomas, the final step in this campaign to see woman's role as that of a sexual servant to male needs was to take away from women any interest in sex. Lacking this interest, a woman posed still less of a threat to the husband's notion that her body was for his sexual pleasures alone.[14]

Thomas' account is psychologically perceptive, but it does not explain the whole story. For one thing, the idea of women as morally pure made easy sexual use of women more difficult rather than less so. Purity gave women grounds for denying the use of their body to their husbands and for resisting the attempt of men to have sex with them outside marriage.[15] Furthermore, the conception of women as sexual property is a very old one. Thomas himself offers an illustration from the reign of the English king Ethelbert, a law which conceived of the sexual services of women as a form of property. One must therefore ask why the notion of female purity, so well developed in the eighteenth and nineteenth centuries, did not develop earlier. It was well within the imaginative powers of earlier generations of men to elaborate an idea of female purity if it had served their interests to do so. In fact, quite the opposite was true: throughout much of the Western Middle Ages, when women were seen as a form of property, they were also generally seen as the lustier sex.

Exactly the same question must be asked of Poovey, who offers a variant of Thomas' argument. The social, economic, and legal setting of eighteenth-century England, she says, perpetuated "among the middle and upper classes the attitude that women were counters to be used in negotiating [marriages] rather than individuals deserving of choice."[16] It was convenient, then, that women should be seen as having no sexual desires of their own. Moreover, the aspiration of the English middle class, she says, was a dynastic one: "to found a family, to endow them splendidly enough to last for ever, and to enjoy a vicarious eternal life in the seed of one's loins."[17] What greater threat to this ambition could there be than a wife's infidelity, which could give as heir to her husband not a true son but a bastard? To the extent that women adopted a belief in their own natural lack of interest in sex, it could only help to reduce men's anxiety on this vital point.

Poovey's arguments suffer from the same weakness as Thomas': none of the general features of the marriage market or inheritance which constrained daughters and wives in the eighteenth century are at all novel to that time. How, then, can they be used to account for the rise of the idea of female purity? What is distinctive about the period is the growth of the demand for and possibility of moral self-control, which created new burdens for male and female members of the culture. The belief in exemplary female morality was one response.

The notion that the rise of the idea of female purity must primarily have served the interests of only one gender is turned to different purposes by Nancy Cott, who sees the asexual character of female purity, which she calls "passionlessness," as serving only women's interests: "The positive contribution of passionlessness was to replace that sexual/carnal characterization of women with a more spiritual/moral one." This belief was "the cornerstone of the argument for women's moral superiority, used to enhance women's status and widen their opportunities" in a world controlled by men.[18]

There is no doubt that Cott is correct. The idea of female moral purity *was* used by women to raise their status and power in a male-dominated world, but this is only a partial explanation of the origin of this idea. Cott does not adequately develop an account of why eighteenth-century men were willing to agree to this conception of women. Why would they wish to do so, and why, in particular, would they idolize and elevate to such a high moral plane women who were pure in this way? Could it be because of their own belief in the high moral worth of a thoroughgoing and fully formed morally constant temper?

Many historians now recognize that the patriarchal culture of eighteenth- and nineteenth-century England (patriarchal to the extent that men were given great authority over women in both law and custom) was nonetheless a culture in which women were seen more and more as the fullest embodiments of conscience. As time goes on, the belief in women becomes amplified in the idea of the moral mother, an idea which has been well articulated by Ruth Bloch in "American Feminine Ideals in Transition: The Rise of the Moral Mother, 1785–1815." Bloch writes that prior to the late eighteenth century, two almost mutually exclusive ideal images of women appeared in the literature written and read in America. The first was that of women as helpmeets. The second was an idea of ornamental refinement, "feminine graces" and "the charms of female social companionship in polite company."[19]

But she points out that in the late eighteenth century a new theme came into play, the theme of the woman as mother, as moral mother—the instructor and creator of conscience in her children. Bloch offers a number of illustrations of this idea, which she sees already developed in the second part of *Pamela*. In this book, Pamela is shown in a variety of situations as a truly moral mother, someone concerned about the moral growth of her children, who instructs them by telling moral fairy tales and who illustrates morality by her own degree of self-sacrifice for her children.

In his advice to mothers, William Buchan says, "Everything great or good in future life, must be the effect of early impressions: and by whom are those impressions to be made but by mothers, who are most interested in the consequences? Their instructions and example will have a lasting influence and of course, will go farther to form the morals, than all the eloquence of the pulpit, the efforts of schoolmasters, or the corrective power of the civil magistrate, who may, indeed, punish crimes, but cannot implant the seeds of virtue."[20]

Before the late eighteenth and early nineteenth centuries, however, this moral educative function belonged to the father. But in time, Bloch writes, some advice books went so far as to make the reverse point, that "fathers should not simply leave the rearing of children entirely to mothers alone." This emphasis on the mother's role in caring for children and in creating their moral outlook is something which Carl Degler has called the "doctrine of the two spheres" or "separate spheres."[21] This was a division of labor in which men's work was largely outside the home and women's work largely within the home; such an arrangement was conceived of primarily as moral and nurturing.

How can we account for the rise of this new ideal at the end of the eighteenth and the beginning of the nineteenth centuries? There is certainly a material basis. Bloch writes that the specialized maternal role is a consequence of the gradual physical removal of the father's place of work from the home, a process already underway in eighteenth-century America among tradesmen, craftsmen, manufacturers, and professionals. The same process was rapidly accelerating in England with the beginning of industrialization. More of the child-rearing was left to mothers; they had more time for it since "women were becoming less vitally engaged in economic production," less involved in home manufacture for domestic use, as more goods became easily available on the commercial market.[22] Bloch thinks that this material change led to the conviction that women were emotionally and morally suited to the rearing of children.

There is no doubt that the division of labor within and outside the home helped to advance the idea of the moral mother, but this conception had an opportunity to grow precisely because there had already been a well-developed conception of female purity in the eighteenth century. When this division of labor came about, there was an opportunity to see women as the natural educators and moral creators of children. Bloch points out that the elevation of women in the late eighteenth and early nineteenth centuries was often associated with a high valuation of their emotionality. This is true; women were seen as morally superior partly because of their capacity for sentiment. Yet the task which was given to women in eighteenth- and nineteenth-century culture was to create self-discipline in their children, both male and female. The idea of women as emotional thus had to be balanced with the idea of women as teachers of restraint and self-denial.

In *Education of the Senses*, Peter Gay makes the point that for many upper-class bourgeois families, the father was the bringer of pleasure, the liberator from rules, and the maker of holidays. Gay quotes from the memoirs of Dora Montefiore, who recalls her early childhood in the 1850s: "Every evening we were dressed to go down to the drawing room for the children's hour, from six to seven, when my dear father had returned home, and we small people were made joyful by his sunny smile and the way in which he entered into our fun and games and devised glorious surprises for us." On Sundays there was what Montefiore called "the pure pagan joy" of a walk with her father.[23]

This account suggests that the belief, associated with the everyday understanding of the Oedipus complex, that the nineteenth-century conscience had its major origin in the relation between children and their fathers needs to be revised. It may have been that much of the burden of transmitting conscience from generation to generation was seen as woman's work, work to be done at home, and that fathers played a more pagan role than we ordinarily assume.

The ideal of the pure woman and moral mother clearly

has affinities with the medieval cult of the Virgin Mary, mother of God. The doctrine of the immaculate conception, asserting that Mary was born without original sin, "provided late medieval theology with a symbol for the original or unfallen state of humanity," writes Rosemary Radford Reuther.[24] Mary also represents mercy and forgiveness. The devotion to Mary, writes Reuther, is in part a reaction to the medieval tendency to exalt Christ as the stern judge of the final Judgment. As Christ becomes the symbol of "guilt and justice," Mary, "like an understanding mother," makes "allowances for the inadequacies of sinful humanity."[25] Feminine forgiveness of men's sinfulness is no stranger to Victorian mythology, and many of the medieval elements of Mariolatry find their secular counterparts in the ideas of the pure woman and the moral mother of eighteenth- and nineteenth-century Protestant culture.

The similarities can easily be overemphasized, however, for the medieval Mary was never made a thoroughly and constantly sexual being, as Pamela was. The eighteenth century created such a woman in response to the claims of the potent conscience. Mary still lived within the ever-repeated cycle of sin, guilt, and repentance.

In *Sincerity and Authenticity*, Lionel Trilling attempts to trace the history of some major themes in the development of European ideas of the moral self from the eighteenth century to the present day. Not surprisingly, he begins with what I have identified as the morally constant self. The sincere self represents itself as it really is. The good faith of modern sincerity, says Trilling, requires a self which is single and steady in its concerns and direction. Only then can it represent itself as it really is. This requirement can be seen, he thinks, in the eighteenth-century use of "the word 'self' not as a mere reflexive or intensive, but as an autonomous noun referring, the *O.E.D.* tells us, to 'that . . . in a person (which) is really and intrinsically *he* (in contradiction to what is adventitious).'"[26] To be a self in this sense, one must be one thing and not many things, steady and not changeable.

Much of Trilling's text is devoted to a study of attacks against this idea of the self in the name of what he calls authenticity. From the point of view of the authentic self, the moral and emotional constancy exhibited by modern civilized men and women is a lie, or at least a distressing diminution of human potential. We are or should be many things, many selves, like Rameau's nephew. Trilling thinks that spokesmen for the disintegrated consciousness arise in the modern world as a reaction to what are felt as the inhumane and falsifying constraints of constancy. He thus continues the story I have told. Just as the oscillating and fluctuating temperament was rejected in the name of constancy, so constancy is rejected in the name of human authenticity. Modern authenticity, of course, is not the same as the oscillating temper described by Huizinga. Authenticity defines itself in opposition to the modern ethic of constancy; the oscillating temperament of the medieval world did not. But the call to authentic selfhood obviously has affinities with the older tradition and in some cases is directly linked to that tradition, as it is in much of nineteenth-century Russian literature.

I have focused for the most part upon the significance of the ethic of constancy for intimate and sociable relations in England, but the demand for constancy is relevant to other historical topics—for example, industrialism—and, as my mention of Russian literature suggests, to other locales. Since Weber's *Protestant Ethic and the Spirit of Capitalism*, historians, sociologists, and economists have debated the place of Western religion in the rise of capitalism and industrialism. Weber argues for the decisive role of religious ideas (as embodied in social practices) in the creation of the modern economic order. The evidence I have presented supports his view.

One of the most commonly remarked features of the industrial order is the requirement of unremitting constancy in the discipline of work. Puritanism much preceded the growth of the English and American industrial order, and it would be absurd to attribute the triumph of this order to Puritanism alone. However, Weber is right to this extent: the rising industrial order of England was able to make use of an ethic and techniques well suited to its own needs, although they had not been designed specifically to meet those needs.[27] A similar tale can be told about France and Germany, although in both countries the development of a social ethic of constancy, and then of industrialism, occurs later than it does in England.[28]

In the United States, the conviction that erotic delight and spontaneity between spouses are not fundamentally hindered by the restraints of constancy continues to be widely promoted. Indeed, constancy is often said to be a route to true and healthy erotic satisfaction. Perhaps the notion has its origins in Puritan culture, with its belief in the possibility and desirability of the integration of ethical and carnal elements in marriage. It is a commonplace of nineteenth- and twentieth-century America that the family is a haven in a heartless world, an island of ease and sweetness amid an unforgiving world of commerce and industry. But perhaps for many it has been the other way around: doing well in business is easy compared to what is expected of one at home, where the demand for the integration of erotic and moral elements looms so large. Work is a respite from a home which asks for more than is possible.

The Puritan notion of marriage may also account for some of the popularity of psychoanalysis and allied therapies in the United States. Men and women turn to these in the hope that they will be able to meet the demands of marriage or similar nonlegal relations more successfully.[29] It is curious that American psychotherapy, so often seen as hostile to "Puritanism," in fact often serves this Puritan end. For some, indeed, therapy becomes the test of whether a marriage should continue. If a marriage is troubled, one or both spouses seek therapy; if, after due time, they still cannot provide each other with the needed warmth and comfort, a divorce seems justified, for they believe that nothing more can be done. The temperamental failings lie too deep to be cured.

The call to an ethic of constancy is not unique to Western

European culture and its descendants. It is a striking feature of Bolshevism, which put itself squarely against the emotional variability and undisciplined spontaneity so well described by nineteenth-century Russian authors, who typically saw emotional steadiness as a distinctively German trait, alien to the Russian soul.[30] Though the lack of self-control and steadiness was often lamented, it was also celebrated as superior to the pettiness of the modern West.

There can be no freedom of soul, no gaiety, no spontaneity, in the reliable life which you demand of yourself and guarantee to your master, says the young Russian moujik to the German peasant boy in the dialogue between the two written by Mikhail Saltykov. But there are no misunderstandings in our life, replies the German. My parents do what they are supposed to, and *Mein Herr* pays them. They have a contract. You have sold your soul for a penny, replies the Russian. Unpredictability, the moujik implies, is at the core of the soul's freedom. I, too, he says, have given up my soul to my master, but there is a difference: I haven't sold it, and so I can take it back.[31] Self-control and reliability for others are not so firmly part of the Russian social order that they cannot be withdrawn by the individual at will. The Russian knows he has freedom, and it permits him to be joyous. The German has lost it and must be excluded—as the German boy is—from the pleasure (and the prospect of the pleasure) of emotional abandon. It is true, the Russian says, we have nothing except joy.[32]

Saltykov's dialogue did not concern itself with sexuality, but obviously the Russian boy's rejection of a thorough moral self-discipline and his espousal of spontaneity should have as much bearing on ideas of erotic life as it does on attitudes toward work and authority. How did the idea and experience of "the Russian soul" affect the Russian experience and conception of sexuality? One would expect that it allowed Russians to maintain a version of the traditional idea that sexual love burns intensely but does not last; this is indeed a theme of much nineteenth-century Russian poetry.

German-speaking culture, on the other hand, has a central role in the development of the idea that sexuality is a constantly active force in the psyche, and surely this can be understood in light of the extraordinary demand for moral self-regulation in many milieus of late nineteenth- and early twentieth-century Germany and Austria. The hope of an integration of conscience and sexuality seems to have fared less well there than in the United States.[33] In the art and the intellectual productions of twentieth-century Germany and Austria, the conviction that one must choose between erotic self-expression and ethical constancy is well developed. Marriage with the thought of ethical responsibility for one another until death, writes Weber, is a form of life alien to passionate sexuality.[34] Freud's belief in the general inadequacy of marriage for the erotic needs of men and women is well known. The same conviction is also evident in *Die Strasse* and *Die Freudlose Gasse*, two "street films" of the 1920s, as well as in *Der Blaue Engel* (1930). After the Second World War, the same theme runs through *Das Mädchen Rosemarie* (1958).[35]

In the well-known concluding passage of *The Protestant Ethic and the Spirit of Capitalism*, Weber writes that in his times, steady, self-disciplined, and unceasing labor—the work ethic—has lost all spiritual, moral, and cultural sense. It is now simply required by capitalism for its own purpose, the production of material goods. For Richard Baxter, says Weber, "[t]he care for external goods should only lie on the shoulders of the 'saint like a light cloak, which can be thrown aside at any moment.'" But fate, Weber adds, "decreed that the cloak should become a housing hard as steel."[36]

How correct is this harsh judgment of constancy in work? As Weber himself knew, the Puritan demand for emotional and moral constancy was by no means limited to the arena of work. Puritans called for a self-disciplined, purposive, steady, ethical self in all areas of life. Weber's readers can easily recognize that his texts are often the product of extraordinarily disciplined and steady inquiry. He himself must have been aware just how much his own writing was the outcome of his own work ethic, indeed, the outcome of his own general commitment to a self-disciplined moral and emotional constancy in all the areas of his life. Did he mean to condemn his own books and articles as products of a culturally and spiritually senseless constancy?

Perhaps he did. The ordinarily unbridgeable divide he felt between joyous and spontaneous erotic love on the one hand and the commitments of ethical constancy on the other insured a deep ambivalence about both dimensions of life. "A housing hard as steel" expresses Weber's sense of the inexpressiveness of constancy. It is not flexible; it has none of the lightness and delicacy which would permit nuanced erotic communication. Wilhelm Reich's term *character armor* suggests that it would be appropriate to liken Weber's hardened steel casing to a suit of armor.[37] The suit of constancy gives a steady shape to one's life—too rigid a shape, Weber implies. It annihilates any possibility of a spontaneous, passionate, and erotic contact with others. The shape one gives to one's life turns out to be a prison or, as the American translator of *The Protestant Ethic*, Talcott Parsons, put it, an "iron cage."[38]

Unsurprisingly, Weber's conviction in the all but necessary chasm between eros and constancy mirrors his own personal experience, in this case, the conflict between the values of his mother and father.[39] His mother gave herself thoroughly to the fulfillment of the ethical tasks of daily life. The ruthless work schedule which Weber had already adopted while a university student, according to Arthur Mitzman, was an expression of Weber's own loyalty and sympathy to his mother's morally demanding way of life.[40] Her favorite theologian was William Ellery Channing, and according to her daughter-in-law, Marianne Weber, the doctrine which Channing preached was simply this: "We grasp God not in ecstatic emotionalism, but in the fulfillment of clear and simple duties: 'The sacrifice of a desire to the will of God is more important than all raptures.' Highest good is the moral energy of holy resolve, spiritual freedom. Its essence is: to be master over the senses, to be master over the material, to be master over fate, over all fear, over custom, independent of every authority."[41]

Weber's father, on the other hand, had much of the pagan quality which Gay sees in many nineteenth-century patriarchs. The elder Max Weber's orientation toward pleasure, power, and a more morally relaxed outlook made him spiritually distant from his wife, who in Marianne Weber's words, found it "increasingly difficult to approach her husband with her own spiritual and religious interests—for they are basically not vital needs for him, and worldly life, office, politics, socialization demand his time."[42] Once again, the woman bore the burden of conscience and of the transmission of conscience to her children. The consequence of this for Weber was a split between his own conscience and eros which he expressed so well, though inappropriately, in his treatment of Puritan culture.

For the Puritans, conscience was not a peculiarly feminine attribute. Puritan men do not appear to have characteristically faced, as many nineteenth-century men did, the challenge of a revolt against the iron cage of the mother in order that their erotic life might have freer expression.

The division of emotional labor in *Pamela* announces a new phase of Western moral history. Women become the bearers of the full message of conscience—and the fullness of sexuality. Before the First World War, one alternative to Weber's Heidelberg, with its high and pressing standards of morality, was Berlin's amoral world of political power. But another, as Martin Green makes clear, was the bohemia of Munich's Schwabing, which so exalted the superior eroticism of women.[43] The primacy of the oedipal revolt against the father in the moral development of the bourgeois male is a contemporary historical and psychological commonplace —and perhaps a reinforcement of the fantasy that sons, and civilization in general, owe all to the fathers, if not in identification then in rejection. Freud's advocacy of the idea may well express his own revolt against the bourgeois belief that the full power of both morality and sexuality in civilization was to be found not in the fathers but in the hearts, minds, and bodies of mothers.

Notes

INTRODUCTION

1. Weber (1958), 119.

2. The ancient philosophers' belief that self-control benefited the individual who possessed it by giving him a certain mastery over himself contrasts sharply with a view of self-control which had developed by the seventeenth century. In this view, self-control is still a benefit to the possessor, but it is a defensive mechanism: it is an asset in a world of active or potential enemies who are kept loyal only by their own self-interest and who may at any time turn out to be enemies. Lawrence Stone cites Sir William Wentworth's advice to his son Thomas, the future Earl of Stafford, written in 1607. Wentworth makes it clear that the only safe way to maneuver through the world is by exercising extreme self-caution, outward reserve, secrecy, and even duplicity: "Be very careful to govern your tongue, and never speak in open places all you think. . . . But to your wife, if she can keep council (as few women can) or to a private faithful friend, or some old servant that hath all his living and credit under you, you may be more open" (Stone [1979], 78).

3. *Spectator* No. 100, 1:420.

4. *Spectator* No. 424, 3:590–92. For further descriptions of the inhabitants of this infirmary, see *Spectator* No. 429, 4:7–11 (Steele) and No. 440, 4:46–48 (Addison).

5. Two texts stand out as insightful introductions to Puritan

theories of marriage: Levin Schücking's *The Puritan Family* and William and Malleville Haller's "The Puritan Art of Love." For criticisms of the claim of Schücking (and others) that Puritan views on marriage were novel, see Todd and Davies.

6. Rogers, 150.

7. Baxter (1678), 2:42; Gataker (1620), 44.

8. Proverbs 5.15, 18–19. For a similar use of this passage, see Griffith, 280–81, 286, and Baxter (1678), 2:42.

9. Baxter (1678) 2:43; Gataker (1620), 37. For similar remarks see Gouge, 239–43.

10. See also Gataker (1620), 44, and Gouge, 207.

11. Rogers, 156.

12. Gouge, 208–09. For a similar passage, see Gataker (1620), 44.

13. In examining the family unit of the period, one sees a parallel tension between spontaneity and moderation. Lawrence Stone notes that English family structure at the upper levels underwent several major changes between 1500 and 1700. Among these changes was a rise in "the importance of affective bonds to tie the conjugal unit together" (Stone [1975], 93). Stone does not appear to see, however, the degree to which new forms of self-control had to be developed in order to make these affectionate elements steady and reliable.

14. Freud (1963), 252–62.

CHAPTER 1

1. Cassirer, 49. Along with Cassirer's and Patrides' texts, Gerald Cragg's *From Puritanism to the Age of Reason* remains a useful introduction to the study of the place of the Cambridge Platonists and Latitudinarians in the creation of the English Enlightenment.

2. Cassirer, 45–46.

3. *Enneads* 5.3.17.

4. Patrides, 18.

5. Smith (1673), 20.

6. Ibid.

7. Ibid., 143–44.

8. Ibid., 7, 9.

9. Patrides, 200, 211. This is from Discourse 13 in More (1692), reprinted in Patrides, 200–12.

10. Patrides, 212.

11. More's *Enchiridion Ethicum* was first published, in Latin, in

1688. Several sources give other dates of first publication; I follow the *Short-Title Catalogue*. It was published in an English translation, entitled *An Account of Virtue*, in 1690. I quote from the second, corrected, edition of this translation (More [1701]), 6–8.

12. Cudworth, 16.

13. Ibid., 18–19, 59–60.

14. Ibid., 40–41.

15. Whichcote, Aphorisms 927, 925 and 1007, quoted in Patrides, 334–35.

16. Whichcote (1751), Discourse 48, 2:385.

17. Aquinas, *S.T.* 2a2ae 47–56. See also Gilby.

18. Quoted in Patrides, 18 n. 3.

19. Smith (1673), 15, 10; Patrides, 18 n. 3.

20. "Eight Letters," Whichcote (1753), 4.

21. Bercovich, 18, quoting Puritan divines.

22. Bercovich, 19. The poem is Goodwin's "Auto-Machia."

23. Smith (1673), 10. "The holy spirit does not descend [*shora*, encamp] on a prophet when he is sad, lazy, giddy, lightheaded, or engaged in petty matters or empty conversation, but rather comes to him when he is engaged in the joyful [willing] performance of a commandment" (Shabbath 30b). It is clear from the Talmudic passage that we might well look to Judaism for some of the sources of the Platonists' ideas. For an excellent introduction to some of the complexities of the notion of the joyful performance of God's commands in Judaism, see Muffs.

24. For Protestant Germany, see Kittsteiner; for Catholic France, see Groethuysen.

25. Butler, Bishop of Bristol at the time, is reported to have stopped suddenly while walking in the palace garden one evening to ask, "What security is there against the insanity of individuals? The physicians know of none!" He continued, after a pause, "[T]hen may not whole communities and public bodies be seized with fits of insanity as well as individuals? Nothing but this principle can account for the major part of those transactions of which we read in history" (Butler, 1:xv).

26. Solzhenitsyn, 35.

27. The "Russian way," which surely has its analogues in other civilizations, has its sympathizers in the West. The conservative Gerhart Niemeyer, professor of political science at the University of Notre Dame, decries "modern nihilism," which includes the philosophies of Turgot, Hegel, Marx, and Comte, as well as the ar-

tistic schools of Fauvism, Cubism, Futurism, Constructivism, Surrealism, Dada, New Realism, and Pop Art. He writes:

> There is one contemporary example, one is tempted to say paradigm, of a return from modern nihilism achieved not primarily by an intellectual effort or by way of the myth, but rather as the result of personal primary experience. It is the case of hundreds, maybe thousands of Soviet labor camp prisoners who were driven to the brink of personal annihilation and regained the reality of man in the reality of transcendence through a spiritual wager of their life. . . . In these cases the road proved viable because at the outset there was not a mere intellectual decision but a totally renewing experience of militantly accepted suffering in soul, body, and mind. One is driven to the conclusion that as deep a loss of reality as modern man experiences cannot be retrieved at any lower cost. (Niemeyer, 345)

28. Miller (1954), 8, 9.

CHAPTER 2

In the preparation of this chapter, I have benefited from F. W. Garforth's intelligently edited and abridged version of Locke's *Some Thoughts Concerning Education* (Locke, 1964).

1. Schochet, 6.
2. Cotton, 4, quoted in Morgan, 19.
3. See Schochet, 78–81.
4. Brailsford, 40, quoted in Schochet, 80–81.
5. Gouge, 10.
6. Quoted in Stone (1975), 55.
7. Ibid., 54, 24.
8. Ibid., 55.
9. Locke (1968), 38.
10. Ibid.
11. Ibid., 45.
12. Ibid., 47.
13. *Thoughts* was first published in 1693. I quote throughout from James Axtell's edition (Locke [1968]), which is based on the fifth edition, published in 1705, the last to undergo revisions by Locke, who died in 1704. I refer to sections of *Thoughts* for the convenience of readers who do not have ready access to Axtell's text.
14. *Thoughts*, secs. 103–04, 38, 35. Where practical, subsequent references to this work are given parenthetically in the text.
15. For an informative study of one Puritan family's treatment of its children, see Nicholas Canny's study of the Boyle family.

16. *Oxford English Dictionary*, s.v. "ingenuous"; see also Garforth's commentary in Locke (1964), 60.

17. *Thoughts*, The Epistle Dedicatory, sec. 216.

18. Ibid., secs. 216, 141–43; see also sec. 94.

19. See "Some Thoughts Concerning Reading and Study for a Gentleman," in Locke (1968), 397–404.

20. *Thoughts*, sec. 94. "*Wisdom* . . . in the popular acceptation," writes Locke, "is a Man's managing his Business ably, with foresight in this World" (sec. 140).

21. Locke (1968), 344.

22. *Treatises* II, secs. 55–57, 64, 173, 174. Locke's *Two Treatises* was first published in 1689, with a publication date of 1690 on the title page. I quote throughout from the Peter Laslett's edition of the treatises (Locke [1963]), which is based on the third printing (1698), as corrected by Locke. "II" indicates the *Second Treatise*. I refer to the section numbers rather than to pages of Laslett's edition for the convenience of readers using other editions.

23. *Treatises*, II, secs. 59, 149–51, 55. Where practical, subsequent references to this work are given parenthetically in the text.

24. Ibid., II, secs. 77–86; see also sec. 2.

25. Ibid., II, sec. 52. Sir Robert Filmer's works in support of a patriarchal theory of government were first published in the 1640s and 1650s. They were republished by the Tories in 1679 and 1680 during the Exclusion Crisis and were the object of Locke's attack in his *First Treatise*. See Laslett's introduction to Locke (1963), 15–161.

26. Ibid., II, sec. 64; see also sec. 66.

27. Ibid., II, secs. 173, 119–22.

28. For one Puritan discussion of marriage as a contract, see Rogers, 96–126. A careful reading of Locke's statements on marriage is found in Shanley.

29. *Treatises*, II, secs. 78, 80; see also I, secs. 91–93.

30. *Treatises*, II, sec. 81. Locke's view is a version of an argument rejected by the young Thomas Aquinas in his commentary on the sentences of Peter Lombard (*Scriptum in IV Libros Sententiarum* 4.33.2.1): "The union of man and woman in marriage is chiefly directed to the begetting, rearing, and instruction of offspring. But all things are complete by a certain time. Therefore after that time it is lawful to put away a wife without prejudice to the natural law." Thomas replies, "By the intention of nature marriage is directed to the rearing of offspring, not merely for a time,

but throughout its whole life. Hence it is of natural law that parents should lay up for their children, and that children should be their parents' heirs." Because sustaining the welfare of children is not a limited task of marriage but a permanent one, husband and wife "must live together for ever inseparably." The strain of individualism in Locke's thought surfaces in his unwillingness to have parents bound by obligations to their children throughout their lives; just as children must become free of parents, so parents must become free of children. The realities of English life, in Locke's time, however, often made grown children of the better classes very much dependent upon their parents' goodwill.

31. Locke (1678), 199, quoted in Laslett's edition of *Treatises* (Locke [1963]), 364, note to sec. 81.

32. See Edmund Leites (1978).

CHAPTER 3

1. Huizinga, 10.
2. Ibid., 11, 14, 12.
3. Petit-Dutaillis, 5, quoted in Elias, 200.
4. Elias, 200. Lawrence Stone concurs:

Such personal correspondence and diaries as survive suggest that social relationships from the fifteenth to the seventeenth centuries tended to be cool, even unfriendly. The extraordinary amount of casual inter-personal physical and verbal violence, as recorded in legal and other records, shows clearly that at all levels men and women were extremely short-tempered. . . . Friends and acquaintances felt honor bound to challenge and kill each other for the slightest affront, however unintentional or spoken in the careless heat of passion or drink. (Stone [1979], 77)

5. Weber (1958), 119.
6. *Spectator* No. 143, 2:65, and No. 424, 3:591. *The Spectator* was published in folio half-sheets from 1711 to 1741; the first collected edition, which contains authorial revisions, appeared in 1712–15. I quote throughout from Bond's critical edition (1965).
7. *Spectator* No. 143, 2:65.
8. *Spectator* No. 381, 3:429. As an epigraph to these remarks, Addison offers a passage from Horace (*Odes* 2.3.1–4) in which the poet calls for an even mind in every state.
9. *Spectator* No. 128, 2:8–9.
10. *Spectator* No. 520, 4:350–51. The original letter (now found

in the Blenheim Palace Archives) is printed in Bond's edition of *The Spectator* (5:236–37). Steele's version clearly reveals his commitment to the ethic of good humor.

11. *Spectator* No. 208, 2:314–15.

12. *Spectator* No. 100, 1:420.

13. *Spectator* No. 143, 2:65.

14. *Spectator* No. 381, 3:430, and No. 100, 1:421.

15. See *Tatler* No. 192, 4:14–19, and *Spectator* No. 268, 2:544–48.

16. Steele (1932), 26–27. *The Christian Hero* was first published in 1701. I quote throughout from Blanchard's critical edition.

17. *Tatler* No. 49, 1:402. *The Tatler* was published in folio half-sheets from 1709 to 1711; I quote from the first collected edition (1710–11), which contains authorial revisions.

18. *Tatler* No. 159, 3:291.

19. Sennett, 18–19, 91.

20. *Tatler* No. 217, 4:157.

21. *Spectator* No. 438, 4:39.

22. *Tatler* No. 172, 3:367–69.

23. Thomas Tickell writes that a steady and uniform "Good-nature . . . accompanied with an Evenness of Temper . . . is, above all things, to be preserved in this Friendship contracted for Life. . . . *Socrates,* and *Marcus Aurelius,* are Instances of Men who, by the Strength of Philosophy, having entirely composed their Minds and subdued their Passions, are celebrated for good Husbands, notwithstanding the first was yoked with *Xantippe,* and the other with *Faustina*" (*Spectator* No. 607, 5:75–76). Steele tells us that Socrates formed himself "for the world by Patience at home" (*Spectator* No. 479, 4:199).

24. *Spectator* No. 144, 2:70.

25. *Tatler* No. 217, 4:157.

26. On the use of feminine charm, see *Spectator* No. 520, 4:351.

27. *Spectator* No. 178, 2:202.

28. Steele (1932), 28.

29. *Spectator* No. 178, 2:202.

30. The campaign of Steele and others to weaken the financial power of women met with some success; see Habakkuk.

31. *Tatler* No. 199, 4:55.

32. *The Tender Husband,* I.ii (Steele [1971], 226).

33. *Tatler* No. 199, 4:57.

34. *Tatler* No. 223, 4:192. See also the remarks of Sir John Bevil

and Humphrey on Bevil Junior's use of the estate he came into by virtue of his parents' marriage settlement, in *The Conscious Lovers*, I.i (Steele [1971], 308).

35. *Tatler* No. 217, 4:161.

36. Huizinga, 26.

37. Erasmus (1957), 15–17.

38. Ibid., 18.

39. Elias, 64.

40. Both regulations quoted in Elias, 131.

41. *De civilitate morum puerilium*, first published in 1530; quoted in Elias, 130.

42. Jean-Baptiste de La Salle, 45ff., quoted in Elias, 132.

43. Elias, 57, 56.

44. *De civilitate*, quoted in Elias, 90.

45. Courtin, 127, quoted in Elias, 92.

46. *De civilitate*, quoted in Elias, 90.

47. Steele was not the first to apply the principles of social individuation to questions of social life; there is a long literature before him, the origins of which seem to be Italian. A notable example is Castiglione's *Il cortegiano*.

CHAPTER 4

1. Weber (1958), 119.

2. Ibid., 53.

3. Those who were Puritan in the ways described divided on the details of their ethics, belief, rite, and piety, and on other matters as well. The legitimacy of clerical authority and, more generally, of all hierarchies of wealth and power was a great point of contention. For an interesting discussion of this issue at the end of the interregnum, see Reay. For a discussion of the meaning of *Puritan* in the sixteenth and seventeenth centuries, see Hall. Much can be learned from Kavolis as well.

4. Noonan, 313.

5. Roman Catechism of 1566, 2.8.13, 14, quoted in Noonan, 313.

6. *De Genesi ad Litteram Libri Duodecim* 9.7.

7. In *De Bono Coniugale* 3.3, Augustine writes that the marriage of old people must have some purpose other than procreation; that purpose is the good of "mutual companionship between the two sexes" *(in diversu sexu societatem)*. This notion of companionship as a good is omitted, however, in his general statements in this work concerning the good of marriage. See Noonan, 127–28.

8. *Nichomachean Ethics* 1162a15–20; *Politics* 1253a5–10.

9. *Nichomachean Ethics* 1162a25–30.

10. It lives, too, in Noonan's *Contraception*, an excellent and subtle work.

11. *Summa Contra Gentiles* 3.124, 3.123.

12. *De Bono Coniugale* 16.18.

13. Quoted in Noonan, 311.

14. Noonan, 326.

15. Ibid., 276.

16. 1518; I quote from the English translation of 1530.

17. Erasmus (1530, sigs. A5v–[A7r]. Although this work was first printed on 30 March 1518, Telle says: "En fait la publication de l'*Encomium Matrimonii* ne date pas de mars 1518," for in some form or other, "l'opuscule était connu en manuscrit depuis plus de vingt ans et courait de mains en mains à travers toute l'Europe" (155). Where practical, references to Erasmus (1530) are given parenthetically in the text.

18. Even the English do, says Erasmus (see Telle, 165), but Tavernour does not include this wisecrack in his translation. Telle thinks that this passage suggests that the *Encomium* "a été remanié en Angleterre au contact du groupe Colet, Latimer, Linacre, More. En cette fin de XVᵉ et debut de XVIᵉ siecle, il appert que la question du mariage était un des sujets les plus débattus outre-Manche. . . . C'est dans ce pays où la question du célibat, du mariage et surtout des mauvais mariages parait avoir été à l'ordre du jour" (165 n. 28, 179). For Telle's evidence for the English influence on Erasmus' views on marriage, see especially 179–80.

19. Todd, 18, 21.

20. Ibid., 32; Telle, 462.

21. Bellarmine, 257–58. Telle thinks that Erasmus works out his anticelibatarian views in terms of "le paulisme matrimonial" (458), but he provides plenty of evidence to link them to a philosophy of what is natural and proper to humankind, a philosophy alive in Aristotle, Thomas, the late medieval theologians I mention above, and the Italian and Northern humanists. Telle writes that Erasmus "n'a jamais écrit ni pensé cette phrase-ci par exemple[:] 'Quod naturae est, imputatur a malo' " (180). Would this be any less true of Thomas?

22. See Schücking; Haller and Haller.

23. Rogers, 9; Gouge, 242, 123. Jeremy Taylor, who was close to the Puritans on many matters concerning marriage, does not share

their estimation of celibacy (Taylor [1650], 81–82). He is closer to Bellarmine. A chaste widowhood deserves praise, Taylor thinks, but the highest esteem must be given to the virginal life. It allows "a perfect Mortification of our strongest appetites" (Taylor [1673], 163). Self-mortification is a well-developed theme in both the Puritan and the Roman Catholic worlds of the sixteenth and seventeenth centuries, but the Puritans do not make much of it through the denial of the sexuality which belongs to marital love. The Puritans call for an integration of the sexuality of husband and wife with other elements of the good and holy life. They therefore reject the admiration of sexual self-mortification found in the Roman Church of the sixteenth and seventeenth centuries in authors as different as Ignatius of Loyola and Pascal.

Baxter's case is instructive. Unlike most Puritans who wrote about marriage, and in spite of the spiritual support he received from his wife, he thought the single life generally more suitable to the three main ends of the Christian life: to "serve God," to advance our "spiritual welfare," and to increase our "Holinesse." Yet Baxter does not praise those who choose the chaste single life for its renunciation of sexuality, nor does he list the sexual aspect of marriage as one of its spiritual disadvantages. In the main, his objection is that marriage creates so many worldly cares and concerns that it easily impedes both the active and the contemplative elements of the Christian life, a theme well known in the writings of the Roman Church, but linked in that tradition to praise of sexual renunciation (Baxter [1678] 2:3–12).

24. Gouge, 123.

25. See Gouge, 121, Ames, 197, and Rogers, 6. Secker writes, "One of the Popes of *Rome*, sprinkles this unholy drop" upon marriage: "*carnis polutionem & immunditiem.* It's strange," says Secker, "that that should be a pollution, which was instituted before corruption; or that impurity, which was ordained in the state of innocency" (17).

26. Secker, 15.

27. Gouge, 122.

28. Ibid.

29. Baxter (1678), 2:40.

30. Gataker (1624), 8.

31. "XV Sermons," Taylor, (1673), 165.

32. Baxter (1678), 2:41.

33. See Gataker (1620), 37.

34. See above all Rogers, 313; also Perkins, 3:691; Griffith, 289; and Milton (1645a), 335. For further documentation of the place of sexual love in marriage as it is seen by Puritans who affirm its place in no uncertain terms, see Frye.

35. Hutchinson, 18–19.

36. Ibid., 10.

37. Ibid., 15.

38. The literature of knightly romance—*Amadis of Gaul* and the like—so popular in Elizabethan and Stuart England even among the pious, also taught the Puritans something about the passion of love (see Wright [1935]). Such literature is less in evidence in seventeenth-century New England, though it is by no means absent (see Wright [1957], 141–44). For an amusing use of the literary style of the romance in early-eighteenth-century New England, see the journal of Sarah Kemble Knight, first published in 1825; for a twentieth-century edition, see Knight (1972). A lively excerpt is published in Miller and Johnson, 2:425–47.

The literature of romance as developed in the more refined forms of English poetry may also have played a part in encouraging the flowering of romantic notions of marriage love among the Puritans. John Leverett, later to be president of Harvard College, copied out several stanzas from Cowley's "Elegie upon Anacreon" and "The Mistress" while still a student. Elnathan Chauncy, son of Harvard's President Charles Chauncy, copied out lyrics of Herrick (including most of "Gather ye rosebuds while ye may") and Spenser, devoting twenty pages of his notebook to Spenser (Morison, 46–52). For the Spenserian background of Milton's thoughts on marital love, see Haller (1946). For a complex and sophisticated discussion of ideas of marriage, love, and sexuality in Spenser and Shakespeare, see Watkins.

39. Perkins, 3:689, 691, 671.

40. Baxter (1678), 2:42.

41. Ibid., 6.

42. With respect to sexuality in marriage, Baxter is thus sometimes close to Richard Allestree, the author of *The Practice of Christian Graces; or, The Whole Duty of Man*, an enormously popular guide to conduct in late-seventeenth-century England, the England of the Restoration. Allestree writes that in *"lawful marriage . . . men are not to think themselvs let loose to please their brutish appetites, but are to keep themselves within such rules of moderation, as agree to the ends of Marriage, which [are] . . . the*

begetting of children, and the avoiding of fornication" (168–69, quoted in Schücking, 23).

43. Weber (1958), 97, 238; Haller and Haller, 243.

44. Weber (1958), 263–64 n. 22.

45. I do not mean to imply that Weber's own sense of the place of erotic passion in life is identical to that of the Puritans. For the fortunate, Weber thinks, there exists a life of desire, love, and passion beyond the realm of reason and cultural demands, tragic in its irrationality yet profoundly sustaining in its meaning. He stresses, in un-Puritan fashion, the ineluctable and tragic conflict between the claims of authentic erotic love and those of rational culture; see Green.

Bertrand Russell's mother and father, if we can trust Russell himself, exemplify the "moderns" of Weber's time who made sexuality a merely medical, physiological, or hygienic phenomenon, a purely "rational" matter. In his autobiography Russell writes that his parents obtained for his brother "a tutor of some scientific ability," who was, however, "in an advanced state of consumption. . . . Apparently upon grounds of pure theory, my father and mother decided that although he ought to remain childless on account of his tuberculosis, it was unfair to expect him to be celibate. My mother therefore, allowed him to live with her, though I know of no evidence that she derived any pleasure from doing so" (1:17).

46. Baxter (1678), 2:43.

47. Ibid., 2:18–31; idem (1681), 307.

48. Gouge, 138–39.

49. Baxter (1681), 70–71.

50. Gataker (1620), 1.

51. See, for example, Rogers, 200, 304–06. Gataker writes: "*A meeke and quiet spirit, in a woman* especially, *is a thing,* saith *Saint Peter, much set by in Gods sight*" ([1624], 20, quoting I Peter 3.4). See also Ames, 156, and Rogers, 236–53.

52. See Rogers, who quotes Paul (I Timothy 5.8): "He that provides not for his family, hath forsaken the faith, and is worse than an Infidell" (220). For Rogers' extended reproof of improvident husbands, whom he divides into nine sorts, see 230–36. See also 288–96.

53. Gataker (1624), 18–19.

54. Baxter writes that he "never knew" the "equal" of his wife's

reason in *"prudential practical"* matters: "in very hard cases, about what was to be done, she would suddenly open all the way that was to be opened, in things of the Family, Estate, or any civil business. And to confess the truth, experience acquainted her, that I knew less in such things than she; and therefore was willing she should take it all upon her" ([1681], 67).

55. Taylor (1684), 53–55. Ames tells us that a husband "ought to reckon of his Wife in all things, as his neerest Companion, and as part of himselfe, or of the same whole, in a certaine parity of honour" (156).

56. *De Amicitia* 8.28–9.30.

57. *Tusculan Disputations* 4.33.70–71.

58. Ibid., 4.33.70.

59. Ibid., 4.31.65–4.33.71.

60. Ibid., 4.17.38–39, 4.32.68.

61. In answer to a letter from Appius Claudius Pulcher, who has just returned to Rome, Cicero writes, "At last, after all, I have read a letter worthy of Appius Claudius—a letter full of kindly feeling, courtesy, and consideration *[plenas humanitatis, offici, diligentiae]*. Evidently the very sight of your urban surroundings has given you back your pristine urbanity" (*Ad Familiares* 3.9.1). Brunt writes that *sermo* (conversation), *litterae* (letters, in the broad sense), and *humanitas* were recognized in Cicero's Rome "as qualities which might make even a disreputable man a welcome associate on whom the name of friend could be bestowed" (5).

62. Taylor (1684), 18–19.

63. Montaigne, 136–37 (*Essays*, 1:28).

64. Thus, for Martial, the difficulty of gaining a woman makes her attractive; there must be some difficulty, else no desire can arise: "You are the paramour of Aufidia, and you were, Scaevinus, her husband; he who was your rival is her husband. Why does another man's wife please you when she as your own does not please you? Is it that when secure you can't get an erection?" (*Epigrams* 3.70). For further examples of the same strain of thought, see *Epigrams* 1.57 and 1.73.

65. Montaigne, 138 (*Essays*, 1:28).

66. For a recent edition of Hutchinson's memoirs, which were written after her husband's death in 1664 but not published until 1806, see Hutchinson.

67. Nelson (1969), 139–64.

68. 1524; quoted in Nelson (1969), 152.
69. Raleigh, 2:351–52, quoted in Nelson (1969), 147–48.
70. Nelson (1974), 94–95.
71. *De Amicitia* 10.35–12.44.
72. Weber (1958), 166–67.
73. Ibid., 105.
74. Ibid., 105–06, 224 n. 30.
75. Ibid., 106–07.
76. Ibid., 105.
77. Ibid., 118–19.
78. Ibid., 154.
79. Rogers, 156.
80. Ibid., 147.
81. Ibid., 147–48; see also Gataker (1623), 11–12.

82. Baxter writes, *"Next to the fear of God, make choice of a nature, or temperament that is not too much unsuitable to you.* A crossness of Dispositions will be a continual vexation: and you will have a Domestick War instead of Love" ([1678], 2:12). Yet he does not praise, as Rogers does, the mysterious source of the love of a man and a woman which leads them to wed: "To say *you Love,* but you *know not why,* is more beseeming Children or mad folks, than those that are soberly entring upon a change of life of so great importance to them" (Baxter [1678], 2:10).

83. The Puritan casuists (except Milton) thought that although temperamental affinity was of prime importance in the choice of a partner, a man had no right to divorce because he made a bad choice; see Gataker (1620), 35, and Johnson, 107–12. Milton went a daring step further. Like his Puritan colleagues, he believed that a fundamental purpose of marriage is mutual support and comfort. He therefore concluded that if differences in temperament between spouses make the fulfillment of this purpose impossible, divorce ought to be permitted to offer the opportunity of remarriage to both parties; he leaves it up to the husband alone to decide whether a divorce shall occur, however. To yoke together a man and a woman who cannot give each other the warmth and comfort that marriage should give condemns them to a miserable life; to force them to maintain such a union defeats the purpose of marriage itself. See Milton (1645a, 1645b, and 1645c) and Milton's edition of Bucer's work on divorce (Bucer). See also Haller and Haller (1941–42) and Haller (1946).

84. Gouge, 133–34.

85. Baxter (1678), 2:41. From the point of view of Kant and many contemporary moral philosophers, *ought* implies *can.* Thus, love is beyond the rule of morals if it is beyond our control. But Puritans sometimes say that if you are unfortunate enough to choose a mate who does not suit your temperament, you must strive to achieve what is beyond human power: you must bring yourself to love a spouse who does not suit you. Gataker tells those who have married one they cannot love "to strive even to enforce their affections; and crave grace at Gods hand, where by they may be enabled to bring themselves to that disposition, that God now requireth" ([1620], 35). In matters of feeling, mood, temperament, motivation, and character, the Puritans saw us as under obligations we might not be able to fulfill without the aid of God's grace, which none of us can command. It should not be supposed that they held this view just to make us acutely aware of our unavoidable sinfulness. On the contrary, it was because of their belief that *ought* need not imply *can* that many Puritans had such an acute sense of sin.

86. Weber (1958), 171, 169, 276 n. 80.

87. Freud (1963), 126, 132.

88. Weber (1958), 119.

89. On integration as a formative principle of the Puritan personality, see Barbu, 145–218.

90. Ibid., 126. For an astute analysis of the different psychologies of enjoyment and excitement, see Tomkins (1962–63 and 1979).

91. For a recent defense of the view that fantasies of aggression are usually required for sexual excitement, see Stoller.

CHAPTER 5

1. In the first mention of a play, and sometimes in subsequent citations, I provide its original year of production in brackets; the new year is considered to begin on January 1. Parenthetical references are to act, scene, and line.

2. The husband, bored with the sweet fruits he once so ardently desired, is a "type" in late-seventeenth-century comedy. For more such husbands, see Southerne, *The Wives Excuse* [1691], I.i.62–65, and Vanbrugh, *The Provok'd Wife* [1697], I.i.

3. See also Etherege, *She Wou'd if She Cou'd* [1668], II.i.

4. See the portrait by the studio of Peter Lely (National Portrait Gallery), reproduced opposite p. 31 in Dryden. For another excel-

lent use of the allure of a masked woman (indeed, of *two* masked women) see *She Wou'd if She Cou'd.*

5. The pleasures of the hunt are not reserved for one sex, for in this sport between men and women, the pursued can take as much pleasure in the course as the hunter, and both may find the match of wits exciting, no matter how the hunt concludes. See *She Wou'd if She Cou'd,* II, i.

6. See also the dialogue between Jacinta and Wildblood in Dryden, *An Evening's Love,* II.i.122–31.

7. See also *An Evening's Love,* III.i.654–59, and Etherege, *The Man of Mode* [1676], III.iii.41–75.

8. See, for example, Sedley, *The Mulberry Garden* [1668], II.i.78–206.

9. Dryden gives us Quintilian in the original: *sunt, enim, longe venustiora omnia in respondendo quam in provocando* (*Institutio Oratoria* VI.iii.13). John Harrington Smith titled his book on the witty lady and the gallant in late-seventeenth-century comedies *The Gay Couple in Restoration Comedy,* but to call them gay today would be misleading.

10. See Ehrmann.

11. See also the dialogue between Wildish and Gertrude in *Buryfair,* IV.[ii].

Negative feelings can also be expressed by saying that one does not want a thorough devotion. A heart that cannot be wholly captured makes excitement possible. At the end of Etherege's *The Man of Mode,* Dorimant offers "infallible" proof to Harriet that he loves her:

> I will renounce all the joys I have in friendship and in Wine, sacrifice to you all the interest I have in other Women——
> HARRIET. Hold——though I wish you devout, I would not have you turn Fanatick. (V.ii.143–47)

She would not have his heart so completely lost in love for her.

12. Where the idea that marriage threatens the excitement of liberty is only weakly developed, a proviso scene can concern itself largely with other matters; see the dialogue between Merryman and Thisbe in Sedley, *Bellamira* [1687], III.ii.75–193.

13. See also Congreve, *The Way of the World* [1700], IV.i.180–209.

14. For my own contribution to the study of autonomy in seventeenth-century England, see Edmund Leites (1974–75 and 1978). See also Dunn (1968 and 1980).

15. Wildish declares that his love has made Gertrude his master, but she doubts that her freedom would survive their marriage. "You are resolv'd to use your Soveraign Power over me," says Wildish, "and I'll show you my Passive Obedience."

> Do you Swagger like a Tyrant? you shall find I can bear like a Slave.
> GERTRUDE.   Yes, you can act a Slave for a time, in hopes of making me one every after. (*Bury-fair*, III.i)

Once again, a woman's at least apparent unwillingness to give up her freedom makes her attractive. In the end, however, Shadwell makes her more interested in submission and devotion than excitement. "And know," she tells Wildish, whose proposal she at last accepts, "for all my vapouring, I can obey, as well as e'er a meek, simpering Milksop on 'em all; and have ever held *Non resistance* a Doctrine fit for all Wives, tho for nobody else" (V.i).

The date of the first performance of this play (1689) no doubt gave Gertrude's lines more punch. She turns out to be, at least in her last lines, a Whig in politics but Tory at home. It would be of interest to divide the actual (as well as theatrical) Whigs of the 1680s and 1690s by their politics of the family.

CHAPTER 6

1. For studies of the Puritan expectations of moral self-regulation in the social forms of adult life, see Woodhouse and the earlier work of Jellinek on Congregationalism and ideas of communal self-government. The Puritans are deservedly well known for their use of law and public opinion as means of restraint upon individual action, but their reliance on these forms was often matched by their expectation of a high degree of self-regulation.

2. See Kittsteiner, 957–59.

3. Although the first edition of *Pamela* was published November 1740, it was dated 1741.

4. See Utter and Bridges.

5. I quote throughout from the useful text of the first edition, prepared by T. C. Duncan Eaves and Ben D. Kimpel (Richardson [1971]). Subsequent references to this edition are given parenthetically in the text.

6. "Perhaps," Pamela says, in another moment of reflection, "this new Condition may be subject to still worse Hazards than those I have escap'd," but she then makes herself a source of these

risks: she would be in danger, "were Conceitedness, Vanity, and Pride, to take hold" of her "frail Heart" (279).

7. For an analysis of Richardson's use of clothes in this novel, see McIntosh.

8. "Great and good God!" Pamela prays, "as thou hast enlarged my Opportunities, enlarge also my Will" to dispense to others "a Portion of that Happiness which I have myself so plentifully receiv'd" (303).

9. For a superb "double reading" of *Clarissa* (Richardson's second novel), see Traugott.

10. This may well account for the novel's appeal to the Marquis de Sade.

11. The social structure of the modern West has been shaped in notable ways by nonhierarchical ideas, for egalitarian notions have played a dramatic and powerful role in Western European culture and its overseas extensions since the seventeenth century. But the anthropologist Louis Dumont has rightly called for caution in the use of these ideas to describe Western society, for the modern world, even with its egalitarian ideology, is still shaped by ideas of hierarchy and purity. (Dumont [1976, 1978, 1979, 1980]). This is nowhere more evident than in the new roles given men and women in the eighteenth- and nineteenth-century English-speaking world.

12. The sense of hypocrisy in *Pamela*, pointed out by Fielding in his satirical *Shamela*, comes from the belief that Pamela's conscience is no more than a smoke screen for her own ambition. The demand for a thorough moral constancy in children may well create this hypocrisy. Locke supposes spirit to be so innate in children that it will survive and even flourish even though they are taught with some force "that they were not to have any thing, because it pleased them, but [only] because it was thought fit for them" (*Thoughts*, sec. 38). One possible outcome is a child who unconsciously transforms what he desires into a goal which his conscience requires him to seek, and he is thus free to give all his energies to its attainment. To those from other cultures and civilizations, where a transformation of desire and self-assertion into duty is perhaps less readily achieved, this psychology may seem like sheer hypocrisy. "The results of this approach have often produced astonishment in the non Anglo-Saxon world" (Schücking, 15). A Lockean upbringing, however, also encourages one to tailor desire so that it can become the voice of reason. Conscience will surely have a say in how far desire can speak in its own voice.

Locke's theory of parenthood is particularly suited to effecting a political and economic order which relies upon individual self-restraint and willingness to act within the forms of law; at the same time, the theory expects a considerable degree of self-seeking and self-assertion in the name of civic, legal, and moral duty. It should therefore come as no surprise that Lockean principles of child-raising were popular in eighteenth-century England, which, speaking very generally, had such an order.

13. Poovey, 15.
14. Douglas (1966), 40.
15. Ibid., 4.
16. Douglas (1975), 50.

CONCLUSION

1. Foucault, 63.
2. Montaigne, 137, 616 (*Essays*, 1:28 and 2:2).
3. Montaigne, 137 (*Essays*, 1:28).
4. Richardson called his sequel *Pamela* as well, distinguishing it from the first volume by subtitling it *the second Part*. The sequel was published in 1741.
5. Foucault, 66.
6. Ibid., 6.
7. Ibid., 61.
8. Tentler, 90, 88.
9. Ibid., 91.
10. Quoted in ibid.
11. Ibid.
12. Greven, 12, 143.
13. Ibid., 14.
14. Thomas, 215, 213.
15. See Cott, 233.
16. Poovey, 13.
17. Ibid., 248 n. 6; Poovey quotes from Perkin, 85.
18. Cott, 233.
19. Bloch, 103.
20. Ibid., 112. The book was itself published in 1804.
21. Bloch, 114; Degler, 8, 9.
22. Bloch, 114, 115.
23. Gay, 102.
24. Reuther, 54.
25. Ibid., 52.

26. Trilling, 25.

27. The enforcement of the demand for constancy upon a population quite antagonistic to it is the bitter tale told by E. P. Thompson in *The Making of the English Working Class.*

28. See Kittsteiner and Groethuysen.

29. See Hale.

30. See Nathan Leites (1953), 186–248. The Russians of today still fear the reliability of their colleagues or subordinates at work. In a more recent study, Leites (1982) points out that the Soviet military views spontaneity and lack of perseverance as major threats to the armed forces.

31. Saltykov, 59.

32. Ibid., 55.

33. For an excellent and novel study of the relations between conscience and sexuality in early-twentieth-century Germany, see Green.

34. Weber (1946), 350.

35. On the movies of the 1920s and 1930s, especially the street movies, see Kracauer.

36. Weber (1958), 181. Following Mitzman (172), I have altered Parson's translation of this passage by substituting the literal and more accurate "a housing hard as steel" for Parson's "iron cage."

37. I owe this insight to Joseph Maier.

38. Weber (1958), 181.

39. This is one of Mitzman's theses in *The Iron Cage.*

40. Ibid., 48.

41. Quoted and translated in Mitzman, 29.

42. Quoted and translated in ibid., 21.

43. Green, 3–100. For some provocative comments on the place of Schwabing in German—and specifically Nazi—history, see Sombart.

Bibliography

[Allestree, Richard.] 1659. *The Practice of Christian Graces; or, the Whole Duty of Man.* London.

Ames, William. 1643. *Conscience, with the Power and Cases thereof.* London: I. Rothwell et al.

Barbu, Zevedei. 1960. *Problems of Historical Psychology.* New York: Grove.

Baxter, Richard. 1678. *A Christian Directory.* 2d ed. 4 vols. London: Nevil Simmons.

———. 1681. *A Breviate of the Life of Margaret, the Daughter of Francis Charlton . . . and Wife of Richard Baxter.* London: B. Simmons and Brabazon Aylmer.

Bellarmine, Robert. 1604. *An Ample Declaration of the Christian Doctrine.* Translated by Richard Hadock. [Douai].

Bercovich, Sacvan. 1975. *The Puritan Origins of the American Self.* New Haven: Yale University Press.

Bloch, Ruth. 1978. "American Feminine Ideals in Transition: The Rise of the Moral Mother, 1785–1815." *Feminist Studies* 4, no. 2:101-26.

[Brailsford, Humphrey.] 1689. *The Poor Man's Help.* [London].

Brunt, P.A. 1965. "'Amicitia' in the Late Roman Republic." *Proceedings of the Cambridge Philological Society* no. 191 (n.s., no. 11): 1–20.

Bucer, Martin. 1644. *The Judgement of Martin Bucer, Concerning Divorce.* Translated by John Milton. London: Matthew Simmons.

Butler, Joseph. 1900. *Works.* Edited by J. H. Bernard. 2 vols. London: Macmillan.

Canny, Nicholas. 1982. *The Upstart Earl: A Study of the Social and Mental World of Richard Boyle, First Earl of Cork, 1566–1643.* Cambridge: Cambridge University Press.

Cassirer, Ernst. 1953. *The Platonic Renaissance in England.* Translated by James P. Pettegrove. Austin: University of Texas Press.

Congreve, William. 1967. *Complete Plays.* Edited by Herbert Davis. Chicago: University of Chicago Press.

Cott, Nancy F. 1978–79. "Passionlessness: An Interpretation of Victorian Sexual Ideology, 1790–1850." *Signs* 4:219–36.

Cotton, John. 1656. *Spiritual Milk for Boston Babes.* [Cambridge, Mass.].

Courtin, Antoine de. 1672. *Nouveau traité de la civilité.* 2d ed. Paris: H. Josset.

Cragg, Gerald R. 1950. *From Puritanism to the Age of Reason.* Cambridge: Cambridge University Press.

Cudworth, Ralph. 1647. *A Sermon before the House of Commons: March 31, 1647.* Cambridge: Roger Daniel.

Davies, Kathleen M. 1977. "The Sacred Condition of Equality—How Original Were Puritan Doctrines of Marriage?" *Social History* 2:563–80.

Degler, Carl N. 1980. *At Odds: Women and the Family in America from the Revolution to the Present.* New York: Oxford University Press.

Douglas, Mary. 1966. *Purity and Danger.* London: Routledge and Kegan Paul.

———. 1975. *Implicit Meanings.* London: Routledge and Kegan Paul.

Dryden, John. 1967. *Four Comedies.* Edited by L. A. Beaurline and Fredson Bowers. Chicago: University of Chicago Press.

Dumont, Louis. 1976. *Homo aequalis, I.* Paris: Gallimard.

———. 1978. "La communauté anthropologique et l'idéologie." *L'Homme* 28, nos. 3–4:83–110.

———. 1979. *Homo hierarchicus.* 2d ed. Paris: Gallimard.

———. 1980. "On Value." *Proceedings of the British Academy* 66:207–41.

Dunn, John. 1969. *The Political Thought of John Locke.* Cambridge: Cambridge University Press.

———. 1980. "Individualism and Clientage in the Formation of John Locke's Social Imagination." In *John Locke: Symposium*

Wolfenbüttel 1979, edited by Reinhard Brandt, 43–73. Berlin: Walter de Gruyter.

Ehrmann, Jacques. 1963. *Un paradis désespéré: l'amour et l'illusion dans "l'Astrée."* New Haven: Yale University Press.

Elias, Norbert. 1978. *The Civilizing Process.* Translated by Edmund Jephcott. New York: Urizen.

Erasmus of Rotterdam. 1530. *A Right Frutefull Epystle . . . in Laude and Prayse of Matrymony.* Translated by Richard Tavernour. London: R. Redman.

———. 1957. *Ten Colloquies.* Translated by Craig R. Thompson. Indianapolis: Bobbs-Merrill.

Etherege, George. 1927. *Dramatic Works.* Edited by H. F. B. Brett-Smith. 2 vols. Oxford: Oxford University Press.

Farrand, Max, ed. 1929. *The Laws and Liberties of Massachusetts: Reprinted from the Copy of the 1648 Edition in the Henry E. Huntington Library.* [Cambridge, Mass].

Foucault, Michel. 1980. *The History of Sexuality. Vol. I: An Introduction.* New York: Vintage. This is a translation of *La Volonté de savoir* (Paris: Gallimard, 1976).

Freud, Sigmund. 1961. *Civilization and its Discontents.* New York: W. W. Norton.

———. 1963. *Character and Culture.* Edited by Philip Rieff. New York: Collier.

Frye, Roland Mushat. 1955. "The Teachings of Classical Puritanism on Conjugal Love." In *Studies in the Renaissance* 2, edited by M. A. Shaber, 148–59. New York: The Renaissance Society of America.

Gataker, Thomas. 1620. *Marriage Duties Briefly Couched Together.* London: William Bladen.

———. 1623. *A Good Wife Gods Gift.* London: Fulke Clifton.

———. 1624. *A Mariage Praier.* London: Fulke Clifton and James Bowler.

Gay, Peter. 1984. *Education of the Senses.* New York: Oxford University Press.

Gilby, Thomas. 1967. "Prudence." In *New Catholic Encyclopaedia,* 12:925–28. New York: McGraw Hill.

Gouge, William. 1626. *Of Domesticall Duties.* 2d ed. London: John Beale.

Green, Martin. 1974. *The von Richthofen Sisters.* New York: Basic.

Greven, Philip. 1977. *The Protestant Temperament.* New York: Knopf.

Griffith, Matthew. 1634. *Bethel; or, a Forme for Families*. London: Ro. Allott and Hen. Taunton.

Groethuysen, Bernard. 1968. *The Bourgeois: Catholicism versus Capitalism in Eighteenth-Century France*. New York: Holt, Rinehart and Winston.

Habakkuk, H. J. 1950. "Marriage Settlements in the Eighteenth Century." *Transactions of the Royal Historical Society* (4th ser.) 32:15–30.

Hale, Nathan G., Jr. 1978. "From Berggasse XIX to Central Park West: the Americanization of Psychoanalysis, 1919–1940." *Journal of the History of the Behavioral Sciences* 14:299–315.

Hall, Basil. 1965. "Puritanism: the Problem of Definition." In *Studies in Church History* 2, edited by G. J. Cuming, 283–96. London: Nelson.

Haller, William. 1946. " 'Hail Wedded Love.' " *ELH* 13:79–97.

—— and Malleville Haller. 1941–42. "The Puritan Art of Love." *Huntington Library Quarterly* 5:235–72.

Huizinga, Johan. 1954. *The Waning of the Middle Ages*. Garden City, N.J.: Doubleday & Company.

Hutchinson, Lucy. 1965. *Memoirs of Colonel Hutchinson*. London: Dent.

Jean–Baptiste de La Salle, Saint. 1729. *Les Règles de la bienséance et de la civilité chrétienne*. Rouen.

Jellinek, Georg. 1901. *The Declaration of the Rights of Man and of Citizens*. Translated by Max Farrand. New York: Henry Holt.

Johnson, James Turner. 1970. *A Society Ordained by God: English Puritan Marriage Doctrine in the First Half of the Seventeenth Century*. Nashville: Abingdon Press.

Kavolis, Vytautas. 1982. "Social Movements and Civilizational Processes." *Comparative Civilizations Review* no. 8:31–58.

Kittsteiner, Heinz-Dieter. 1984. "From Grace to Virtue: Concerning a Change in the Presentation of the Parable of the Prodigal Son in the Eighteenth and Early Nineteenth Centuries." *Social Science Information* 23:955–75. This is a translation of "Von der Gnade zur Tugend. Über eine Veränderung in der Darstellung des Gleichnisses vom verlorenen Sohn im 18. und frühen 19. Jahrhundert." In *Spiegel und Gleichnis: Festschrift für Jacob Taubes*, edited by Norbert W. Bolz and Wolfgang Hübener, 135–48. Würzburg: Konigshausen & Neumann, 1983.

Knight, Sarah Kemble. 1972. *The Journal of Madam Knight*. Edited by Malcolm Freiberg. Boston: Godine.

Kracauer, Siegfried. 1947. *From Caligari to Hitler.* Princeton: Princeton University Press.

Leites, Edmund. 1974–75. "Conscience, Casuistry, and Moral Decision: Some Historical Perspectives." *Journal of Chinese Philosophy* 2:41–48.

———. 1978. "Conscience, Leisure, and Learning: Locke and the Levellers." *Sociological Analysis* 39:36–61.

Leites, Nathan. 1953. *A Study of Bolshevism.* Glencoe, Ill.: Free Press.

———. 1982. *Soviet Style in War.* New York: Crane Russak.

Locke, John. 1679. *Diary.* Locke Collection, Bodleian Library, Oxford.

———. 1963. *Two Treatises of Government.* Edited by Peter Laslett. New York: New American Library.

———. 1964. *Some Thoughts Concerning Education.* Edited by F. W. Garforth. Woodbury, N.Y.: Barron's Educational Series.

———. 1968. *The Educational Writings of John Locke.* Edited by James L. Axtell. Cambridge: Cambridge University Press.

Luther, Martin. 1524. "Von Kaufshandlung und Wucher." In *Werke,* edited by J. K. F. Knaacke et al., 15:298–305. Weimar: H. Böhlau et al., 1883–1973.

McIntosh, Carey. 1968. "Pamela's Clothing." *ELH* 35:75–83.

Martial. 1968. *Epigrams.* Rev. ed. 2 vols. Translated by W. C. A. Ker. London: Heinemann.

Mather, Cotton. 1721. *A Course of Sermons in Early Piety.* [Boston].

Miller, Perry. 1954. *The New England Mind: The Seventeenth Century.* Boston: Beacon Press.

——— and Thomas H. Johnson, eds. 1963. *The Puritans.* 2 vols. New York: Harper & Row.

Milton, John. 1645a. *Tetrachordon.* London.

———. 1645b. *Colasterion.* [London].

———. 1645c. *The Doctrine and Discipline of Divorce.* 3d ed. London.

Mitzman, Arthur. 1970. *The Iron Cage.* New York: Knopf.

Montaigne, Michel de. 1958. *Complete Essays.* Translated by Donald M. Frame. Stanford: Stanford University Press.

More, Henry. 1692. *Discourses on Several Texts of Scripture.* Edited by John Worthington. London: Brabazon Aylmer.

———. 1701. *An Account of Virtue; or, Dr. Henry More's Abridgement of Morals, put into English.* 2d ed. London: Benj. Tooke.

Morgan, Edmund S. 1966. The Puritan Family. Rev. ed. New York: Harper & Row.

Morison, Samuel Eliot. 1936. *The Puritan Pronaos*. New York: New York University Press.

Muffs, Yochanan. 1975. "Joy and Love as Metaphorical Expressions of Willingness and Spontaneity in Cuneiform, Ancient Hebrew, and Related Literatures." In *Christianity, Judaism and Other Greco-Roman Cults: Studies for Morton Smith at Sixty*, 4 vols., edited by Jacob Neusner, 3:1–36. Leiden: Brill.

Nelson, Benjamin. 1969. *The Idea of Usury*. 2d ed. Chicago: University of Chicago Press.

———. 1974. "*Eros, Logos, Nomos, Polis:* Their Changing Balances and the Vicissitudes of Communities and Civilizations." In *Changing Perspectives in the Scientific Study of Religion*, edited by Alan W. Eister, 85–111. New York: John Wiley & Sons.

Niemeyer, Gerhart. 1978. "Loss of Reality: Gnosticism and Modern Nihilism." *Modern Age* 22:338–45.

Noonan, John Thomas. 1965. *Contraception*. Cambridge: Harvard University Press.

Patrides, Constantinos, ed. 1969. *The Cambridge Platonists*. London: Edward Arnold.

Perkin, Harold. 1969. *The Origins of Modern English Society, 1780–1880*. London: Routledge & Kegan Paul.

Perkins, William. 1616–18. *Workes*. 3 vols. London: John Legatt et al.

Petit-Dutaillis, Charles. 1908. *Documents nouveaux sur les moeurs populaires et le droit de vengeance dans les Pays-Bas au XVe siècle*. Paris: Honoré Champion.

Poovey, Mary. 1984. *The Proper Lady and the Woman Writer*. Chicago: University of Chicago Press.

Raleigh, Walter. 1751. *Works*. 2 vols. [London].

Reay, Barry. 1978. "The Quakers, 1659, and the Restoration of the Monarchy." *History* 63:193–213.

Reuther, Rosemary Radford. 1975. *New Woman, New Earth*. New York: Seabury.

Richardson, Samuel. 1971. *Pamela*. Edited by T. C. Duncan Eaves and Ben D. Kimpel. New York: Houghton Mifflin.

Rogers, Daniel. 1642. *Matrimoniall Honour*. London: Philip Nevil.

Russell, Bertrand. 1967–69. *Autobiography*. 3 vols. London: George Allen and Unwin.

Saltykov, Mikhail [N. Tchédrine, pseud.]. 1887. *Berlin et Paris: voyage satirique à travers l'Europe.* Translated by Michel Delines [pseud.]. 4th ed. Paris: Louis Westhausser.

Schochet, Gordon J. 1975. *Patriarchalism in Political Thought.* Oxford: Basil Blackwell.

Schücking, Levin Ludwig. 1969. *The Puritan Family.* Translated by Brian Battershaw. London: Routledge & Kegan Paul. This is an English version of *Die Puritanische Familie in literarsoziologischer Sicht.* Berne: Francke Verlag, 1964.

Secker, William. 1658. *A Wedding Ring Fit for the Finger.* London: Thomas Parkhurst.

Sedley, Charles. 1928. *Poetical and Dramatic Works.* Edited by Vivian de Sola Pinto. 2 vols. London: Constable.

Sennett, Richard. 1977. *The Fall of Public Man.* New York: Knopf.

Shadwell, Thomas. 1689. *Bury-fair.* London: James Knapton.

Shanley, Mary Lyndon. 1979. "Marriage Contract and Social Contract in Seventeenth Century Political Thought." *Western Political Quarterly* 32:79–91.

Smith, John. 1673. *Select Discourses.* 2d ed. Cambridge: W. Morden.

Smith, John Harrington. 1948. *The Gay Couple in Restoration Comedy.* Cambridge: Harvard University Press.

Solzhenitsyn, Aleksandr. 1978. *A World Split Apart.* New York: Harper & Row.

Sombart, Nicolaus. 1976. "Gruppenbild mit zwei Damen: Zum Verhältnis von Wissenschaft, Politik und Eros in Wilhelminschen Zeitalter." *Merkur* 30:972–90.

Southerne, Thomas. 1973. *The Wives Excuse.* Edited by Ralph R. Thornton. Wynnewood, Pa.: Livingston.

The Spectator. 1965. Edited by Donald F. Bond. 5 vols. Oxford: Clarendon.

Steele, Richard. 1932. *The Christian Hero.* Edited by Rae Blanchard. London: Oxford University Press and Humphrey Milford.

———. 1971. *Plays.* Edited by Shirley Strum Kenny. Oxford: Clarendon.

Stoller, Robert. 1979. *Sexual Excitement.* New York: Pantheon.

Stone, Lawrence. 1975. "The Rise of the Nuclear Family in Early Modern England: The Patriarchal Stage." In *The Family as History,* edited by Charles G. Rosenberg, 13–57. Philadelphia: University of Pennsylvania Press.

————. 1979. *The Family, Sex and Marriage in England 1500–1800*. Abridged ed. New York: Harper & Row.

The Tatler [The Lucubrations of Isaac Bickerstaff Esq]. 1710–11. 4 vols. London: Charles Lillie and John Morphew.

Taylor, Jeremy. 1650. *The Rule and Exercises of Holy Living*. London: R. Royston.

————. 1673. *Eniautos*. 4th ed. 2 vols. London: R. Royston.

————. 1684. *The Measures of Friendship*. 4th ed. London: R. Royston.

Telle, Emile V. 1954. *Erasme de Rotterdam et le septième sacrement*. Geneva: E. Droz.

Tentler, Thomas N. 1977. *Sin and Confession on the Eve of the Reformation*. Princeton: Princeton University Press.

Thomas, Keith. 1959. "The Double Standard." *Journal of the History of Ideas* 20:195–216.

Thompson, E. P. 1964. *The Making of the English Working Class*. New York: Pantheon.

Todd, Margo. 1980. "Humanists, Puritans and the Spiritualized Household." *Church History* 49:18–34.

Tomkins, Silvan S. 1962–63. *Affect, Imagery, Consciousness*, vols. 1–2. New York: Springer.

————. 1979. "Script Theory: Differential Magnification of Affects." In *Nebraska Symposium on Motivation, 1978*, vol. 26 of *Current Theory and Research in Motivation*, edited by Richard A. Dienstbier, 201–36. Lincoln: University of Nebraska Press.

Traugott, John. 1977. "*Clarissa's* Richardson: An Essay to Find the Reader." In *English Literature in the Age of Disguise*, edited by Maximillian E. Novak, 157–208. Berkeley and Los Angeles: University of California Press.

Trilling, Lionel. 1972. *Sincerity and Authenticity*. Cambridge: Harvard University Press.

Utter, Robert, and Gwendolyn Bridges. 1937. *Pamela's Daughters*. New York: Macmillan.

Vanbrugh, John. 1927–28. *Complete Works*. Edited by Bonamy Dobree and Geoffrey Webb. 4 vols. Bloomsbury (London): Nonesuch.

Watkins, Walter B. C. 1950. *Shakespeare and Spenser*. Princeton: Princeton University Press.

Weber, Max. 1946. *From Max Weber: Essays in Sociology*. Translated and edited by H. H. Gerth and C. Wright Mills. New York: Oxford University Press.

———. 1958. *The Protestant Ethic and the Spirit of Capitalism.* Translated by Talcott Parsons. New York: Charles Scribner's Sons.

Whichcote, Benjamin. 1751. *Works.* 4 vols. Aberdeen: Alexander Thomson.

———. 1753. *Moral and Religious Aphorisms . . . To which are added Eight Letters: which passed between Dr. Whichcote . . . and Dr. Tuckney.* London: J. Payne.

Woodhouse, A. S. P., ed. 1951. *Puritanism and Liberty.* Chicago: University of Chicago Press.

Wright, Louis Booker. 1935. *Middle-Class Culture in Elizabethan England.* Chapel Hill: University of North Carolina Press.

———. 1957. *The Cultural Life of the American Colonies, 1607– 1763.* New York: Harper.

Wycherly, William. 1966. *Complete Plays.* Edited by Gerald Weales. Garden City, N.Y.: Doubleday.

Index